ROMANCE WRITING 101

All Your Questions Answered

HACKNEY AND JONES

Copyright © 2023 by Hackney and Jones

All rights reserved.

No part of this book may be reproduced in any form or by any electronic or mechanical means, including information storage and retrieval systems, without written permission from the author, except for the use of brief quotations in a book review.

Contents

Introduction	v
1. Sub-Genres Of Romance	1
2. The Key Elements Of A Romance Novel	4
3. Biggest Frustrations Romance Writers Face When Writing … And How To Overcome Them	6
4. How Do Romance Writers Make Money?	9
5. Quick Tips For Romance Writers Starting Out	11
6. Popular Romance Novels	13
7. Common Fears When Writing A Novel	15
8. Fears About Writing A Romance	17
9. Romance Writing Mistakes To Avoid	19
10. Romance Fiction Clichés	21
11. What Romance Readers Do And Don't Want	23
12. Romance Writing Checklist	26
13. Sex In Romance Novels	28
14. Plotting Or Pantsing?	30
15. Point Of View In Novel Writing	33
16. Coming Up With A Romance Idea For Your Novel	37
17. Plotting And Structuring Your Novel	40
18. Creating A Compelling Opening Scene	42
19. Creating Characters	44
20. How To Incorporate Emotions In Your Romance Novel	48
21. How To Create A Sense Of Place And Atmosphere In Your Writing	51
22. Plot Twists	53
23. Red Herrings	58
24. Using Descriptive Language	64
25. Writing Dialogue In Your Romance Novel	74
26. How To End Your Novel	89
27. Romance Novel Book Titles	100
28. Romance Writing Word Count	105
29. Romance Fiction Book Cover Tips	106
30. Editors	111

31. Book Marketing	114
32. Romance Writing Glossary	124
Want To Get Your Romance Novel Written?	127

Introduction

In this comprehensive guide, we'll cover everything you need to know to get started with your romance writing career. From the key elements of a romance novel to quick tips for writers starting out, we'll walk you through the process of creating a compelling and successful romance novel.

You'll learn about the most popular romance novels and common fears and mistakes that many romance writers make. We'll also cover what romance readers do and don't want, and provide a romance writing checklist to keep you on track.

In addition, we'll dive into important topics such as sex in romance novels, plotting or pantsing, point of view, creating a compelling opening scene, character development, plot twists, red herrings, using descriptive language, writing dialogue, and how to end your novel. We'll also cover tips for creating romance novel book titles and book covers, as well as working with editors and marketing your book.

By reading **"Romance Writing 101"**, you'll gain the knowledge and tools you need to start writing your romance novel with confidence. Whether you're a seasoned writer or a beginner, this guide will help you avoid common pitfalls and create a compelling and successful romance novel that readers will love. Don't miss out on this invaluable resource for your romance writing journey!

Why we are bringing this book to you

As successful authors who have experienced the ups and downs of the romance writing industry, we know first-hand how challenging it can be to break into the market and create a successful novel. We've made mistakes along the way and have learned valuable lessons that we want to share with you.

That's why we're writing this book - to help you avoid costly and embarrassing errors that can set you back in your writing career. By sharing our experiences, insights, and tips, we aim to help you fast-track your way to success and achieve your dreams of becoming a published romance author.

Whether you're a beginner or a seasoned writer, there's always room for improvement and new knowledge to be gained. Our goal is to provide you with the tools and resources you need to create a compelling and successful romance novel that resonates with readers and establishes you as a trusted and talented author.

We're passionate about helping other writers succeed, and we believe that by reading this book, you'll gain valuable insights and strategies that will help you achieve your writing goals.

So don't let mistakes hold you back - let us help you navigate the romance writing world and make your mark in this exciting and rewarding industry.

Vicky & Claire
Hackney and Jones Publishing

1

Sub-Genres Of Romance

Here are some popular sub-genres of romance fiction and what they are about, along with famous examples and other valuable information about each one:

Contemporary romance: This sub-genre features stories set in the present day and explores modern themes and issues. Examples of contemporary romance novels include **"The Kiss Quotient"** by Helen Hoang, **"The Hating Game"** by Sally Thorne, and **"The Bride Test"** by Helen Hoang.

Historical romance: Set in a historical period, this sub-genre often features aristocratic or wealthy characters and explores societal norms and customs of the time. Examples of historical romance novels include **"Outlander"** by Diana Gabaldon, **"The Duke and I"** by Julia Quinn, and **"The Wallflower Wager"** by Tessa Dare.

Paranormal romance: This sub-genre blends elements of fantasy and science fiction with romance, featuring supernatural characters and themes such as magic, vampires, werewolves, and otherworldly beings. Examples of paranormal romance novels include **"Twilight"** by Stephenie Meyer, **"Dark Lover"** by J.R. Ward, and **"A Discovery of Witches"** by Deborah Harkness.

Romantic suspense: This sub-genre blends elements of suspense and thriller with romance, featuring a hero and heroine who must work together to solve a mystery or defeat a villain. Examples of romantic suspense novels include **"Naked in Death"** by J.D. Robb, **"Gone Girl"** by Gillian Flynn, and **"The Witness"** by Nora Roberts.

Regency romance: Set in the early 19th century in England, this sub-genre features aristocratic or wealthy characters and explores the social customs of the time. Examples of Regency romance novels include **"Pride and Prejudice"** by Jane Austen, **"The Bridgertons"** series by Julia Quinn, and **"A Rogue by Any Other Name"** by Sarah MacLean.

Young Adult romance: This sub-genre is geared toward teenage readers and features characters who are typically in high school or college. Examples of young adult romance novels include **"To All the Boys I've Loved Before"** by Jenny Han, **"The Fault in Our Stars"** by John Green, and **"The Selection"** by Kiera Cass.

Christian romance: This sub-genre features stories that include themes of faith, redemption, and Christian values. Examples of Christian romance novels include **"Redeeming Love"** by Francine Rivers, **"Love Comes Softly"** by Janette Oke, and **"The Shack"** by William P. Young.

LGBT romance: This sub-genre explores relationships between characters who identify as LGBT and includes themes of identity, acceptance, and love. Examples of LGBT romance novels include **"Carry On"** by Rainbow Rowell, **"The Price of Salt"** by Patricia Highsmith, and **"The Seven Husbands of Evelyn Hugo"** by Taylor Jenkins Reid.

Overall, these sub-genres of romance fiction offer a range of themes, settings, and character types, catering to a wide range of readers. Whether you prefer contemporary or historical romance, paranormal or Christian romance, there's a sub-genre out there for everyone.

2

The Key Elements Of A Romance Novel

Romance novels are a popular genre of fiction that typically feature a love story as their central focus. While there is no one set formula for writing a romance novel, there are certain key elements that are commonly found in the genre.

Here are some of the key elements of a romance novel:

A central love story: The primary focus of a romance novel is the romantic relationship between the main characters. This is the heart of the story and what drives the plot forward.

Compelling characters: The characters in a romance novel should be complex and fully developed, with their own backstories and motivations that drive their actions in the story.

Obstacles to love: No romance novel would be complete without some obstacles to the central love story. These could be external obstacles, such as societal or cultural norms, or internal obstacles, such as the characters' own fears or insecurities.

Emotional intensity: Romance novels are known for their

emotional intensity, with the characters experiencing a wide range of emotions as they navigate the ups and downs of their relationship.

Happily ever after (HEA): Most romance novels have a HEA ending, where the main characters end up together and their love is affirmed.

Sensuality: Romance novels can be sensual, with varying degrees of explicitness depending on the sub-genre. However, the focus is typically on the emotional connection between the characters, rather than just physical attraction.

Tension and conflict: A romance novel needs to have tension and conflict to keep the reader engaged. This could be in the form of external conflict, such as the characters being from different worlds or having conflicting goals, or internal conflict, such as personal struggles or emotional baggage.

A sense of hope: Despite the obstacles and challenges, a romance novel should ultimately leave the reader with a sense of hope for love and happiness.

3

Biggest Frustrations Romance Writers Face When Writing ... And How To Overcome Them

Here are the top 10 biggest frustrations that romance writers face when writing, along with actionable steps to overcome them:

1. Writer's block: This is a common frustration for all writers, including romance writers. To overcome writer's block, try setting a writing schedule and creating a writing routine. You can also try writing prompts or free writing exercises to get your creative juices flowing.

2. Lack of motivation: Writing a novel can be a long and challenging process, and it's easy to lose motivation. To overcome this, set realistic goals for yourself and celebrate your achievements along the way. You can also try joining a writing group or community to stay motivated and get feedback on your work.

3. Self-doubt: It's natural to doubt your writing abilities, but it's important to remember that even the most successful writers have doubts. To overcome self-doubt, try practising self-care and focusing on the positive feedback you receive from readers and other writers. You can also seek out support from writing communities or professional writing coaches.

4. Procrastination: It's easy to get distracted or procrastinate when working on a novel, but it's important to stay focused and disciplined. To overcome procrastination, try setting specific goals and deadlines for yourself, breaking your writing into manageable chunks, and using tools like productivity apps or timers to stay on track.

5. Fear of rejection: Rejection is a natural part of the writing process, but it can be difficult to overcome. To deal with the fear of rejection, try reframing rejection as a learning opportunity and focus on improving your craft. You can also seek out support from writing communities or professional coaches to get feedback and improve your writing.

6. Burnout: Writing can be a time-consuming and emotionally draining process, and it's easy to get burnt out. To overcome burnout, take breaks and practise self-care. You can also try working on multiple projects at once or varying your writing routine to keep things fresh and engaging.

7. Perfectionism: It's natural to want your writing to be perfect, but perfectionism can lead to writer's block and other frustrations. To overcome perfectionism, remember that your first draft doesn't have to be perfect, and focus on getting your ideas down on paper. You can also try setting a time limit for each writing session to keep yourself from getting bogged down in details.

8. Lack of inspiration: Sometimes it can be difficult to find inspiration for your writing. To overcome this, try seeking out new experiences or reading books in different genres. You can also try brainstorming or free writing exercises to spark new ideas and keep your writing fresh.

9. Editing overload: Editing is an important part of the writing process, but it's easy to get overwhelmed by the process. To overcome editing overload, try breaking the editing process into manageable chunks and focusing on one area at a time. You can also seek out professional editing services or beta readers to get feedback and improve your writing.

10. Lack of support: Writing can be a lonely process, and it's important to have a support system in place. To overcome this, try joining a writing group or community, attending writing conferences or events, or seeking out support from family and friends who are supportive of your writing goals.

Overall, these frustrations can be challenging, but with the right mindset, tools, and support, you can overcome them and create a successful and engaging romance novel.

Remember, it is natural to feel these things – go easy on yourself.

4

How Do Romance Writers Make Money?

Romance writers can make money through various avenues. Here are a few common ways that romance writers can earn a living:

Traditional publishing: Romance writers can submit their manuscripts to traditional publishing houses, which will pay them an advance and a percentage of the book's sales. The advance is an upfront payment against future royalties.

Self-publishing: With the rise of self-publishing, romance writers can now publish their books themselves through platforms like Amazon's Kindle Direct Publishing. Self-publishing allows writers to retain more control over their work and earn a higher percentage of royalties, but they also have to do more of the marketing and promotional work themselves.

Hybrid publishing: Some publishers offer a hybrid publishing model that combines elements of traditional publishing and self-publishing. Writers pay a fee to have their books published, but they also receive more support with editing, design, and marketing.

Literary agents: Romance writers can work with literary agents, who will help them navigate the publishing industry and negotiate contracts with publishers. Agents typically receive a percentage of the writer's earnings.

Freelance writing: Romance writers can also earn money by writing articles or stories for magazines, websites, or other publications. These gigs may pay a flat fee or a per-word rate.

Speaking engagements: Some romance writers are able to earn money through speaking engagements, book tours, and other public appearances. They may be paid a fee to speak at events, or they may earn money through book sales.

It's worth noting that many romance writers supplement their income with other jobs, as writing can be a difficult industry to make a full-time living in. However, for those who are able to build a loyal following and write consistently popular books, a career as a romance writer can be quite lucrative.

5

Quick Tips For Romance Writers Starting Out

Here are some quick tips for romance writers starting out:

Read widely in the romance genre: To become a successful romance writer, it's important to be familiar with the conventions of the genre. Read widely in the romance genre to get a sense of what works and what doesn't.

Write regularly: The more you write, the better you'll get. Make it a habit to write every day, even if it's just for a few minutes. Set yourself a goal, such as writing 500 words a day, and stick to it.

Join a writing community: Join a writing group or attend a writing conference to connect with other romance writers. These communities can provide valuable feedback and support as you navigate the writing process.

Embrace the editing process: Writing a novel is a long and often difficult process, and your first draft is likely to need a lot of editing. Embrace the editing process and be willing to make changes to your work as needed.

Know your market: It's important to have a good understanding of the market you're writing for. Research what types of romance novels are popular, what readers are looking for, and what publishers are currently acquiring.

Develop strong characters: Characters are the heart of a good romance novel. Spend time developing fully realised, complex characters with unique personalities and motivations.

Create conflict: A good romance novel needs conflict to keep the reader engaged. Identify the obstacles that your characters will face and create tension throughout the story.

Show, don't tell: Rather than telling readers what's happening, show them through the characters' actions, dialogue, and inner thoughts.

Be persistent: Writing is a tough business, and rejection is a common experience for writers starting out. Be persistent and keep submitting your work. Every "no" brings you closer to a "yes."

Have fun: Above all, writing should be a joyous and fulfilling experience. Have fun with your writing and enjoy the process of creating something new.

6

Popular Romance Novels

There are many popular romance novels out there, but here are a few that have gained widespread recognition and acclaim:

"Pride and Prejudice" by Jane Austen - This classic novel follows the tumultuous relationship between Elizabeth Bennet and Mr. Darcy, set against the backdrop of Regency England.

"Outlander" by Diana Gabaldon - This time-travel romance novel follows the relationship between World War II nurse Claire Randall and Scottish Highlander Jamie Fraser.

"Bridgerton" series by Julia Quinn - This series of historical romance novels has gained renewed popularity after the success of the Netflix series adaptation. Set in Regency-era England, the novels follow the romantic escapades of the Bridgerton family.

"The Notebook" by Nicholas Sparks - This popular novel tells the story of a young couple, Allie and Noah, who fall in love in the 1940s and are reunited years later.

"Twilight" series by Stephenie Meyer - This young adult romance series follows the forbidden love between teenage human Bella Swan and vampire Edward Cullen.

"The Fault in Our Stars" by John Green - This bestselling novel tells the story of two teenagers, Hazel and Augustus, who fall in love while navigating the challenges of terminal illness.

"The Time Traveler's Wife" by Audrey Niffenegger - This novel tells the story of Henry, a man with a genetic disorder that causes him to time-travel, and his wife Clare, who must navigate the challenges of their unusual relationship.

"The Hating Game" by Sally Thorne - This contemporary romance novel follows the competitive and tense relationship between coworkers Lucy and Joshua, who find themselves attracted to each other despite their initial dislike

7

Common Fears When Writing A Novel

Fear of failure: Many writers worry that their novel won't be good enough or won't be well-received by readers. To overcome this fear, it can be helpful to remember that writing is a process, and it's normal for first drafts to need a lot of revision. Focus on the joy of writing and the satisfaction of finishing a project, rather than worrying about the end result.

Fear of the blank page: Starting a new writing project can be intimidating, especially when faced with a blank page or screen. To overcome this fear, try breaking the project down into smaller, manageable tasks. Set a goal of writing a certain number of words per day, or write a rough outline of the story to help guide your writing.

Fear of the editing process: Writing a first draft is just the beginning of the process, and many writers worry about the revisions and editing that come next. To overcome this fear, try to approach the editing process with an open mind and a willingness to make changes. Remember that editing is an opportunity to improve the story and make it the best it can be.

Fear of rejection: Once the novel is complete, writers may worry about submitting it to agents or publishers and facing rejection. To overcome this fear, try to remember that rejection is a normal part of the writing process. Don't take rejections personally, and use them as an opportunity to learn and improve your writing.

Fear of exposure: Writing a novel can feel very personal, and some writers may worry about exposing their innermost thoughts and feelings to readers. To overcome this fear, remember that writing is a form of self-expression and that sharing your thoughts and feelings can be a powerful way to connect with readers. Share your work with trusted friends or family members first, and gradually build up your confidence in sharing it with a wider audience.

Fear of success: While it may seem counterintuitive, some writers worry about what will happen if their novel is successful. To overcome this fear, try to focus on the present moment and the joy of writing. Don't worry too much about the future, and remember that success is a journey, not a destination. Enjoy the process of writing and let the future take care of itself.

8

Fears About Writing A Romance

Here are some specific fears a beginner author may have about writing a romance novel, along with tips on how to overcome them:

Fear of writing clichés: Romance is a popular genre, and it can be challenging for a beginner writer to come up with fresh and original ideas. To overcome this fear, try to approach the story from a unique perspective, or think about how you can subvert common romance tropes. You could also try brainstorming with a writing partner or joining a writing group to get feedback and fresh ideas.

Fear of writing explicit scenes: Depending on the sub-genre, romance novels can include sensual or even explicit scenes. This can be intimidating for a beginner writer who may be uncomfortable with writing such scenes. To overcome this fear, start by reading widely in the genre to get a sense of how other writers handle sensual scenes. It may also be helpful to write a rough draft of the scene without worrying about getting it perfect, and then come back to it later to revise and edit as needed.

Fear of writing unrealistic dialogue: Dialogue is an important part of any novel, and it can be challenging for a beginner writer to write dialogue that sounds realistic and natural. To overcome this fear, try to think about how real people talk and interact. You could also try reading your dialogue out loud or having someone else read it to you to get a sense of how it sounds.

Fear of not knowing the genre conventions: Romance has a number of conventions and expectations, such as the importance of the "happily ever after" ending. It can be daunting for a beginner writer to try to navigate these conventions. To overcome this fear, read widely in the genre and pay attention to how other writers handle these conventions. You could also consider working with a writing coach or mentor who is familiar with the genre and can offer guidance and support.

Fear of writing believable characters: Characters are the heart of any good novel, and it can be challenging for a beginner writer to create characters that feel real and three-dimensional. To overcome this fear, start by getting to know your characters inside and out. Develop their backstories, motivations, and personalities, and think about how they will grow and change over the course of the story. You could also try writing character sketches or doing character interviews to get a deeper sense of who they are.

Remember that writing is a journey, and it's normal to experience fear and self-doubt along the way. The key is to keep writing, keep learning, and keep growing as a writer. With persistence and practice, you can overcome these fears and become a successful romance writer.

9

Romance Writing Mistakes To Avoid

Romance writing, like any other genre, has its own set of common mistakes that writers should try to avoid. Here are some romance writing mistakes to watch out for:

Lack of conflict: A good romance novel needs conflict to keep the reader engaged. Without conflict, the story can feel flat and uninteresting. Make sure to include obstacles and challenges that the characters must overcome in order to be together.

Overuse of clichés: Romance is a genre that can be prone to clichés and overused tropes. While some clichés are inevitable in any genre, be careful not to rely on them too heavily. Try to approach the story from a unique perspective and think about how you can subvert common romance tropes.

Lack of character development: Characters are the heart of any novel, and it's important to give them depth and complexity. Make sure to develop fully realised characters with their own backstories, motivations, and personalities.

Unrealistic dialogue: Dialogue is an important part of any novel, and it can be challenging to write dialogue that sounds realistic and natural. Avoid writing dialogue that is overly formal or stilted, and try to think about how real people talk and interact.

Lack of tension: Tension is what keeps the reader engaged and turning the pages. Without tension, the story can feel slow and uninteresting. Make sure to include moments of tension and suspense throughout the story to keep the reader engaged.

Lack of research: Romance novels often have a historical or cultural setting, and it's important to do research to ensure accuracy and authenticity. Make sure to research the time period or culture you are writing about, and strive for accuracy in the details.

Lack of diversity: Romance novels should strive to be inclusive and represent a diverse range of experiences and identities. Make sure to include characters from different backgrounds and with different life experiences.

By avoiding these common mistakes, you can create a more engaging and compelling romance novel that readers will love.

10

Romance Fiction Clichés

Here are the top 10 romance fiction clichés and what you could do instead:

1. Love at first sight: Instead of relying on love at first sight, try developing a deeper, more complex relationship between your characters. You could focus on building emotional connections and creating realistic obstacles to their relationship.

2. The perfect man or woman: Instead of creating perfect characters, try developing flawed and complex characters who are more realistic and relatable. This will make their journey more interesting and engaging for readers.

3. The misunderstanding: Instead of relying on misunderstandings to create conflict in your story, try developing more realistic obstacles that challenge your characters' relationship. You could also focus on creating more complex conflicts.

4. The love triangle: Instead of relying on a love triangle to create drama, try developing more unique and creative conflicts that challenge your characters. You could also focus on creating more complex and realistic relationships between your characters.

5. The happily ever after: Instead of relying on a traditional "happily ever after" ending, try creating more realistic endings that reflect the complexities of real relationships.

6. The alpha male: Instead of relying on the alpha male stereotype, try developing more diverse and complex characters. You could also focus on creating more interesting and realistic power dynamics between your characters.

7. The damsel in distress: Instead of relying on the damsel in distress trope, try developing more independent and strong female characters. You could also focus on creating more interesting and realistic power dynamics between your characters.

8. The rich and powerful: Instead of relying on the rich and powerful trope, try developing more realistic and relatable characters from diverse backgrounds. You could also focus on exploring more nuanced power dynamics between your characters.

9. The big romantic gesture: Instead of relying on big romantic gestures, try focusing on the smaller, more meaningful moments between your characters. You could also focus on creating more nuanced expressions of love.

10. The love-hate relationship: Instead of relying on a love-hate relationship, try developing more complex and realistic relationships between your characters. You could focus on creating greater emotional dynamics and exploring the complexity of human relationships.

11

What Romance Readers Do And Don't Want

This chapter will outline some things that romance readers typically do and don't want in their novels.

What romance readers DO want

Strong, relatable characters: Romance readers want to connect with the characters in the story and feel invested in their journey.

A well-developed romance: The romance is the heart of a good romance novel, and readers want to see a believable and satisfying love story.

Emotional depth: Romance readers want to feel deeply for the characters and be swept up in the emotions of the story.

A satisfying ending: Romance readers expect a "happily ever after" ending, or at the very least, a hopeful and uplifting one.

Tension and conflict: Readers want to be kept on the edge of their seats and feel invested in the outcome of the story.

Diversity and representation: Romance readers want to see characters from different backgrounds and with different life experiences.

What romance readers DON'T want

Misogyny or sexism: Readers don't want to see women portrayed in a negative or degrading light.

Insta-love: Readers don't want to see a romance that develops too quickly or feels forced.

One-dimensional characters: Readers want to see well-developed, complex characters that feel like real people.

Non-consensual sex: Readers don't want to see scenes of non-consensual sex or sexual assault.

Weak female characters: Readers don't want to see female characters who are overly passive or who rely too much on the male protagonist.

Predictability: Readers don't want to see a story that is too predictable or formulaic. They want to be surprised and engaged by the story.

It's important to keep in mind that every reader is different, and what one reader wants in a romance novel may not be the same as what another reader wants. However, these are some general trends and preferences that many romance readers share.

12

Romance Writing Checklist

Develop well-rounded characters: Spend time developing your main characters, giving them unique personalities, motivations, and backstories. Make sure they have flaws and strengths, and that they are relatable to your readers.

Establish the conflict: Every good romance needs conflict. Identify the obstacles that your characters will face and establish them early on in the story.

Create sexual tension: Sexual tension is a key component of a good romance novel. Use dialogue, body language, and other cues to establish a sense of attraction and desire between your characters.

Write a compelling plot: Your plot should be interesting and engaging, with enough twists and turns to keep readers hooked. Make sure that the plot is driven by the characters and their desires and motivations.

Set the scene: Setting is important in any novel, and in a romance novel it can be particularly evocative. Use sensory details to help readers imagine the setting and create a mood or atmosphere.

Write believable dialogue: Dialogue is an important part of any novel, and in a romance novel it can be particularly important for establishing the emotional connection between the characters. Make sure that your dialogue is natural and realistic, and that it reflects the characters' personalities and motivations.

Include physical touch: Touch is an important way to establish a sense of intimacy and connection between your characters. Use physical touch to heighten the sexual tension and emotional connection between your characters.

Create an emotional journey: A good romance should take the reader on an emotional journey. Make sure that your characters experience growth and change over the course of the story, and that their emotions are realistic and relatable.

Avoid clichés: Romance is a genre that can be prone to clichés, such as the "love at first sight" trope. Try to avoid clichés and come up with fresh, original ideas for your story.

Edit and revise: Once you've finished your first draft, be prepared to edit and revise your work. Look for areas where you can tighten up the prose, develop the characters further, or add more tension and conflict.

13

Sex In Romance Novels

Writing about sex in a romance novel can be challenging, as it's important to handle the topic in a way that is tasteful, authentic, and respectful.

Here are some tips for writing about sex in romance novels:

Use sensory details: Sex scenes should be written with sensory details that help the reader visualise and experience the scene. Use all five senses to describe the experience, including the sound of breathing, the taste of sweat, and the scent of perfume or cologne.

Respect consent: It's important to handle the topic of consent carefully in a romance novel. Make sure that both characters are consenting and enthusiastic about the sexual encounter, and that there is a clear understanding of boundaries.

Avoid euphemisms: Use clear and direct language when describing sex scenes. Avoid using euphemisms that may come across as cheesy or unrealistic.

Write from the character's perspective: Write the sex scenes from the character's perspective, focusing on their emotions and reactions. Use their thoughts and feelings to describe the experience, rather than focusing solely on physical descriptions.

Avoid clichés: Avoid clichéd descriptions of sex scenes, such as comparing body parts to flowers or other objects. Instead, focus on unique and original descriptions that feel true to your characters.

Consider the emotional impact: Sex scenes can be a powerful way to deepen the emotional connection between characters. Think about the emotional impact of the scene and how it fits into the overall story.

Consider the audience: Romance novels come in a range of sub-genres, from sweet and clean to more explicit. Make sure to consider the expectations of your intended audience and write the scene accordingly.

Get feedback: Once you've written your sex scene, consider getting feedback from beta readers or a writing group. This can help you get a sense of how the scene is working and whether it's conveying the emotions and impact that you want it to.

By using these tips, you can write sex scenes that feel authentic, respectful, and emotionally impactful.

Remember to approach the topic with care and consideration, and always keep your characters and story in mind.

14

Plotting Or Pantsing?

When it comes to writing a novel, there are two general approaches: plotting and pantsing. This chapter will give a full explanation of each approach, along with their pros and cons.

Plotting

Plotting is a method of writing where the author creates a detailed outline or plan for the story before beginning to write. This can include a chapter-by-chapter outline, character sketches, and other notes to help guide the writing process.

Pros of plotting include:

Better organisation: Plotting can help writers stay organised and on track with their story, making it easier to write a coherent and well-structured novel.

Fewer writer's block: Plotting can help reduce the chances of writer's block, as writers know where the story is headed and can focus on filling in the details.

More efficient: Plotting can be a more efficient method of writing, as writers have a roadmap to follow and don't need to spend as much time figuring out where the story is going.

Cons of plotting include:

Limited flexibility: Plotting can limit the flexibility of the writing process, as writers may feel constrained by the outline and have less room to explore new ideas.

Can feel too structured: Some writers may find plotting too structured or formulaic, leading to a less creative or imaginative end result.

Takes more time: Plotting can take more time and effort upfront, as writers need to create a detailed outline before beginning to write.

Pantsing

Pantsing, also known as "writing by the seat of your pants," is a method of writing where the author starts with a general idea or concept and then allows the story to unfold organically as they write.

Pros of pantsing include:

More creativity: Pantsing can lead to more creativity and spontaneity in the writing process, as writers are free to explore new ideas and take the story in unexpected directions.

More flexibility: Pantsing allows for more flexibility in the writing process, as writers can change direction or try new things without feeling constrained by an outline.

Faster writing: Pantsing can be a faster method of writing, as writers can focus on getting the story down on paper without worrying about details or structure.

Cons of pantsing include:

More writer's block: Pantsing can lead to more writer's block, as writers may not know where the story is going or how to move forward.

Can lead to less structure: Pantsing can sometimes lead to a less structured or well-organised story, as writers may not have a clear sense of the overall plot or direction of the story.

More editing: Pantsing can lead to more editing and revisions later on, as writers may need to go back and add structure or clarity to the story.

Ultimately, the choice between plotting and pantsing is a personal one, and different writers may find that one method works better for them than the other.

Some writers may even use a combination of both methods, starting with a rough outline and then allowing the story to evolve organically as they write. The most important thing is to find a method that works for you and helps you create the best possible novel.

15

Point Of View In Novel Writing

Point of view, or POV, is the perspective from which a story is told.

There are several different types of POV commonly used in novel writing, each with its own benefits and challenges.

Here is a detailed but easy to understand guide to POV in novel writing, along with tips and benefits of each.

First person POV

First person POV is when the story is told from the perspective of the main character, using "I" as the pronoun. Benefits of first person POV include:

Deep emotional connection: First person POV allows readers to get inside the head of the main character, creating a deep emotional connection with them.

Intimate and personal: First person POV can create an intimate and personal feel to the story, as readers experience events through the eyes of the protagonist.

Greater control: First person POV can give the writer greater control over the narrative, as the reader only knows what the protagonist knows.

Tips for writing in first person POV:

Stay consistent with the character's voice: The voice of the protagonist should be consistent throughout the story.

Avoid excessive self-reflection: The protagonist should not spend too much time reflecting on themselves or their actions, as it can become repetitive.

Develop other characters: It's important to develop other characters outside of the protagonist to create a well-rounded story.

Third person limited POV

Third person limited POV is when the story is told from the perspective of a single character, using "he" or "she" as the pronoun. Benefits of third person limited POV include:

Greater flexibility: Third person limited POV offers greater flexibility in terms of the story and the narrative.

Ability to create multiple characters: Third person limited POV allows the writer to create multiple characters with their own unique perspectives and personalities.

Increased objectivity: Third person limited POV offers

increased objectivity, as the writer can create distance between the reader and the protagonist.

Tips for writing in third person limited POV:

Establish the main character early: The main character should be established early on to help the reader identify with them.

Avoid head-hopping: It's important to avoid head-hopping, which is when the writer switches between different character perspectives within a scene.

Use vivid sensory details: The writer should use vivid sensory details to help immerse the reader in the story.

Third person omniscient POV

Third person omniscient POV is when the story is told from the perspective of an all-knowing narrator, using "he" or "she" as the pronoun. Benefits of third person omniscient POV include:

Greater insight into the story: Third person omniscient POV allows the writer to give the reader greater insight into the story and its characters.

Increased flexibility: Third person omniscient POV offers increased flexibility, as the writer can move between characters and events as needed.

Ability to create suspense: Third person omniscient POV can create suspense, as the reader knows more than the characters.

Tips for writing in third person omniscient POV:

Be careful with character knowledge: The writer should be careful with what the narrator knows versus what the characters know to avoid plot holes.

Avoid head-hopping: It's important to avoid head-hopping, which is when the writer switches between different character perspectives *within* a scene.

Use clear transitions: The writer should use clear transitions when moving between different characters or events.

By understanding the different types of POV and their benefits and challenges, writers can choose the best approach for their story and create a compelling and engaging novel.

16

Coming Up With A Romance Idea For Your Novel

Take inspiration from your own life: Draw on your own experiences with love and relationships for inspiration.

Combine different genres: Consider blending romance with other genres, such as fantasy, sci-fi, or mystery.

Take inspiration from real-life stories: Read real-life love stories in the news or online and use them as inspiration for your novel.

Use writing prompts: Writing prompts can be a great way to generate ideas and spark creativity.

Explore different cultures: Explore different cultures and their traditions around love and relationships for inspiration.

Play with opposites: Consider pairing characters who are opposites in personality, background, or values.

Use music as inspiration: Listen to music that evokes a certain emotion or feeling and use it as inspiration for your story.

Explore different time periods: Consider setting your story in a different time period or era, such as the Victorian era or the 1920s.

Use a dream journal: Keep a dream journal and use your dreams as inspiration for your story.

Create a character first: Start by creating a unique and compelling character and build the story around them.

Use setting as inspiration: Choose a unique or interesting setting, such as a small town or a remote island, and use it as inspiration for your story.

Explore different forms of love: Consider exploring different forms of love, such as unrequited love or forbidden love.

Use astrology as inspiration: Use astrology to create unique and interesting character traits or relationships.

Explore different sub-genres: Consider exploring different sub-genres of romance, such as paranormal romance or romantic comedy.

Use mythology as inspiration: Draw on mythology or folklore for inspiration, such as the story of Cupid and Psyche.

Write a retelling: Consider retelling a classic story, such as Romeo and Juliet or Beauty and the Beast, with a unique twist.

Explore different age groups: Consider writing a romance novel that features characters from a different age group than your own.

Use different perspectives: Consider writing from the perspective of a non-human character, such as a ghost or a mermaid.

Use food as inspiration: Use food or cooking as a way to bring characters together and create a unique and memorable romance.

Write from personal ads: Write a romance story based on personal ads or classified ads, either real or fictional.

By using these common and unusual methods, you can come up with unique and interesting ideas for your romance novel that will captivate readers and keep them engaged from beginning to end.

17

Plotting And Structuring Your Novel

Understand the 3-act structure: The 3-act structure is a commonly used structure in storytelling that divides a story into three parts: the **setup, confrontation,** and **resolution.**

- The setup establishes the main characters, their world, and their goals.
- The confrontation presents obstacles and challenges that the characters must overcome.
- The resolution resolves the conflicts and brings the story to a satisfying conclusion.

Develop your characters: Strong characters are essential for any novel, and even more so for a romance novel. Your characters need to be relatable, interesting, and multidimensional. Develop their personalities, motivations, and backstory to create fully fleshed-out characters that readers can care about.

Establish conflict: Conflict is what drives a story forward and creates tension that keeps readers engaged. In a romance novel, the conflict can be external (such as a societal or physical barrier between the main characters) or internal (such as their own personal fears or doubts).

Create a timeline: Once you have your story idea and characters, it's important to create a timeline of events. This will help you organise the plot and keep track of the timing of important events.

Use plot points: Plot points are key moments in a story that move the plot forward and keep the reader engaged. These can include inciting incidents, major conflicts, and the climax.

Focus on the romance: The romance should be the central focus of your story. Make sure you're spending enough time developing the relationship between your main characters and building the tension between them.

Balance pacing: The pacing of your novel is important. Make sure you're balancing scenes of action and conflict with slower, more emotional scenes that allow the characters to develop and the romance to deepen.

Use dialogue: Dialogue is a powerful tool in any novel, but especially in a romance. Use dialogue to reveal character, build tension, and deepen the relationship between your main characters.

Keep it realistic: While romance novels can be fantastical and full of drama, it's important to keep your story grounded in reality. Your characters should have realistic motivations and reactions to events.

Edit and revise: Once you've completed your first draft, take the time to edit and revise. Look for inconsistencies in the plot or character development, and make sure you're telling the story you intended to tell.

18

Creating A Compelling Opening Scene

Start with action: A great way to grab a reader's attention is to start with action. This doesn't necessarily mean a physical action scene, but rather a scene where something is happening that creates tension or conflict.

Introduce your main characters: Your opening scene is a great opportunity to introduce your main characters and give readers a sense of who they are. Make sure to give readers a reason to care about these characters and invest in their story.

Set the tone: Your opening scene should set the tone for your entire novel. If you're writing a light-hearted romance, your opening should reflect that. If you're writing a more dramatic romance, the opening should be more serious.

Create suspense: A great way to keep readers engaged from the very beginning is to create suspense in the opening scene. This can be done by starting with a mystery or a problem that needs to be solved.

Use vivid descriptions: Creating vivid descriptions of the setting, characters, and events can help draw the reader in and immerse them in your story. Make sure to use descriptive language that paints a picture in the reader's mind.

Start in the middle: Instead of starting at the beginning of your story, try starting in the middle of the action. This can create a sense of urgency and make readers want to know how the characters got to that point.

Create emotional stakes: Your opening scene should make it clear what's at stake for your main characters emotionally. This can be a great way to create tension and keep readers invested in the story.

Use dialogue: Dialogue is a great way to reveal character and create tension. Consider starting your novel with a conversation between your main characters that hints at the conflict to come.

Create a sense of place: Your opening scene should give readers a sense of where the story is taking place. Use descriptive language to create a vivid sense of the setting.

Keep it brief: While you want your opening scene to be compelling, you also don't want to overwhelm readers with too much information. Keep your opening scene brief and to the point, with just enough detail to draw the reader in and leave them wanting more.

19

Creating Characters

Establish basic information: Start by establishing basic information about your characters, such as their name, age, gender, occupation, and physical appearance.

Create backgrounds: Create a backstory for each character that explains how they got to where they are in your story. This can include family history, educational background, and career path.

Develop personalities: Give your characters unique personalities that set them apart from one another. Consider using personality tests or character questionnaires to help you flesh out their traits.

Define goals and motivations: Every character should have goals and motivations that drive their actions in the story. Consider what your characters want and why they want it.

Create conflicts: To make your story interesting, create conflicts that challenge your characters and prevent them from achieving their goals. This can include external conflicts, such as a love triangle, or internal conflicts, such as overcoming personal fears or doubts.

Add quirks and flaws: Characters that have quirks and flaws are more interesting and relatable to readers. Consider adding quirks or flaws to your characters that make them more unique.

Build relationships: Relationships between characters are a key aspect of any romance novel. Consider how your characters interact with one another and how their relationships develop over the course of the story.

Use foils: Foils are characters that are opposite in nature and highlight each other's differences. Consider adding a foil character to your story to create more tension and conflict.

Make them dynamic: Dynamic characters change and evolve over the course of a story. Consider how your characters grow and change as the story progresses.

Test your characters: Test your characters by putting them in difficult situations and seeing how they react. This can help you understand their motivations and personalities better.

Example:

Let's say you're creating a character named Sarah. Here are some steps and ideas for developing her:

Basic information: Sarah is a 28-year-old woman with curly brown hair and green eyes.

Background: Sarah grew up in a small town in the Midwest and moved to the city after college. She has a degree in marketing and works as a marketing coordinator for a software company.

Personality: Sarah is outgoing and friendly, but she's also insecure about her appearance. She's a hard worker and is driven to succeed in her career.

Goals and motivations: Sarah's goal is to get a promotion at work, but she also wants to find love and settle down.

Conflicts: Sarah is competing for the same promotion as her co-worker, who is also her ex-boyfriend. She's also struggling to find a good work-life balance and is feeling burnt out.

Quirks and flaws: Sarah is a terrible cook and often burns her meals. She's also self-conscious about her body and has a tendency to compare herself to others.

Relationships: Sarah is close with her best friend from college, who encourages her to pursue her goals. She's also attracted to a new coworker, but is hesitant to start a relationship with him.

Foils: Sarah's ex-boyfriend is her foil, as he's more focused on his career and is willing to do whatever it takes to get the promotion.

Dynamic: Over the course of the story, Sarah learns to stand up for herself and assert her needs at work and in her personal life.

Testing: Sarah is put in a difficult position when she's asked to work on a project with her ex-boyfriend, which tests her ability to remain professional and focused on her goals.

Creating a full character profile for your romance novel

- What is your character's name, age, and physical appearance?
- What is your character's backstory and how does it shape who they are now?

- What are your character's personal strengths and weaknesses?
- What are your character's passions and interests?
- What are your character's goals and aspirations?
- What are your character's fears and vulnerabilities?
- What are your character's values and beliefs?
- What is your character's personality type and how do they interact with others?
- What are your character's likes and dislikes?
- What is your character's family background and relationships with family members?
- What is your character's occupation or profession?
- What are your character's hobbies or pastimes?
- What are your character's romantic and sexual preferences?
- What are your character's most significant life experiences?
- What are your character's flaws and how do they work to overcome them?

Answering these questions can help you create well-rounded, complex characters that readers can connect with and care about. Be sure to also consider how your character's traits, experiences, and relationships will influence the plot of your romance novel.

20

How To Incorporate Emotions In Your Romance Novel

Incorporating emotions is essential to a successful romance novel.

Here are some tips and easy examples to help you incorporate emotions into your romance novel:

Show, don't tell: Instead of telling readers how a character feels, show their emotions through their actions, body language, and dialogue. For example, instead of saying *"Sarah was angry,"* you could show her clenching her fists, glaring at someone, or snapping at them.

Use internal monologue: Internal monologue allows readers to see inside a character's head and understand their thoughts and emotions. Use this technique to show how a character feels about a situation or another character.

Build tension: Build tension between your main characters by creating conflict and obstacles that prevent them from being together. This tension can create a sense of longing and desire that keeps readers engaged.

Use sensory details: Use sensory details to create a vivid sense of the setting and atmosphere. This can help readers feel like they're experiencing the story alongside the characters and can heighten the emotional impact of the story.

Vary emotions: Don't rely on just one or two emotions throughout the novel. Vary the emotions to keep readers engaged and create a more complex and realistic portrayal of the characters.

Use dialogue: Dialogue can be a powerful tool for showing emotions. Consider how the characters speak to one another and how their words reflect their emotions.

Create vulnerability: Vulnerability is a key aspect of any romance. By showing vulnerability, you allow readers to connect with the characters on a deeper level and become invested in their story.

Use subtext: Subtext is the hidden meaning behind what a character says or does. Use this technique to show the characters' true emotions and motivations.

Example:

Let's say you have a scene where Sarah confesses her feelings to her love interest, Tom.

Here are some ways you could incorporate emotions:

Show Sarah's nervousness by having her fidget with her hands or tap her foot.

Use **internal monologue** to show Sarah's thoughts, such as *"I can't believe I'm doing this. What if he doesn't feel the same way?"*

Use **dialogue** to show Tom's surprise or confusion, such as *"I had no idea you felt this way, Sarah."*

Use **sensory details** to create a romantic atmosphere, such as candles flickering and soft music playing.

Vary the emotions by having Sarah feel nervous, excited, and vulnerable all at once.

Use **subtext** to show that Sarah is taking a risk by confessing her feelings, and that Tom's response will determine the future of their relationship.

21

How To Create A Sense Of Place And Atmosphere In Your Writing

Use descriptive language: Use descriptive language to help your readers visualise the scene. For example, if your characters are at a beach, you could describe the sound of waves crashing on the shore, the feel of the sand between their toes, and the salty smell of the ocean.

Consider the setting's role: Think about how the setting can play a role in the story. For example, if your characters are in a cosy café, this could be a place where they feel comfortable and able to connect with one another.

Use details: Use specific details to create a sense of place. For example, if your characters are at a ball, you could describe the way the light catches on the chandeliers, the sound of music filling the air, and the feel of the dancers' dresses brushing against one another.

Use metaphors and imagery: Use metaphors and imagery to create a sense of atmosphere. For example, if your characters are in a dark alleyway, you could describe the shadows as *"clutching at them like bony fingers"* or the dim lighting as *"casting a sickly yellow glow."*

Vary the atmosphere: Vary the atmosphere to create different moods throughout the novel. For example, a sunny park might create a cheerful and romantic atmosphere, while a rainy day might create a more melancholic or introspective mood.

Use the five senses: Use the five senses to create a sense of place and atmosphere. For example, if your characters are at a carnival, you could describe the taste of cotton candy, the smell of popcorn, the sound of carnival games, the feel of the breeze, and the sight of the colourful lights.

Create contrast: Create contrast to highlight the setting and atmosphere. For example, if your characters are in a bustling city, you could contrast the noisy and chaotic streets with a quiet and serene park where they can connect in a more intimate setting.

By incorporating these techniques, you can create a vivid and engaging sense of place and atmosphere in your romance novel that will immerse your readers in the story.

22

Plot Twists

A plot twist is a sudden and unexpected turn of events in a story that catches the audience by surprise. It can be a crucial moment in a novel that can elevate the story and create a memorable experience for the reader.

The impact of a plot twist on an audience can be significant. A well-executed twist can create a sense of shock, excitement, and satisfaction in the reader. It can also add depth to characters, create a shift in the story's trajectory, and generate suspense.

To create a successful plot twist, the writer needs to lay the groundwork for it throughout the story subtly. The twist should be a logical outcome of the events that have transpired, while still being unexpected. This can be achieved through foreshadowing, misdirection, and careful planning.

Some ideas for a plot twist in a romance novel

1. The main character's love interest turns out to be a ghost or an apparition, and they can never be together.

2. The person the main character thought was their soulmate turns out to be a con artist or an undercover agent, sent to spy on them.

3. The protagonist discovers that they are related to their love interest, which complicates their relationship.

4. The love interest has a secret family or a hidden life, which the main character uncovers.

5. The main character realises that their love interest is the one who has been anonymously sending them love letters or gifts all along.

Ultimately, a plot twist can make or break a story, and it's essential to handle it carefully. When done right, it can be a memorable moment that elevates the story and leaves a lasting impression on the reader.

Common types of plot twist

1. The "unreliable narrator" twist, where the perspective of the story is suddenly called into question, and the audience realises that what they thought was true is not. This twist can be effective in creating suspense and adding layers to a character.

2. The "red herring" twist, where the audience is led to believe that one thing is happening or one character is responsible for something, only to discover later that they were wrong. This twist can be used to misdirect the audience and create tension.

3. The "backstory" twist, where the audience learns something about a character's past that changes their understanding of that character or their actions. This twist can be used to add depth and complexity to characters and their motivations.

Actionable steps to create an epic plot twist in a romance novel

Start with a strong foundation: A good plot twist is built on a solid foundation, so make sure your characters are well-developed and their motivations are clear. The more invested readers are in your characters, the more impactful the twist will be.

Identify the common romance tropes: To create a plot twist, you need to know the common romance tropes and expectations that readers have. Once you know these tropes, you can subvert them in unexpected ways to create a twist.

Think outside the box: A good plot twist needs to be unexpected and surprising, so don't be afraid to think outside the box. Consider unexpected character motivations, hidden agendas, or secrets that come to light.

Build tension: A plot twist needs to be well-timed and well-executed to have the most impact. Build tension leading up to the twist by dropping subtle hints and foreshadowing events to come.

Consider the consequences: A plot twist should have consequences that ripple through the rest of the story. Consider how the twist will affect the characters and the story's overall direction.

Make it personal: A plot twist is most impactful when it affects the main character on a personal level. Consider how the twist will affect the character's relationships, goals, or beliefs.

Don't be afraid to revise: A good plot twist takes time to develop and refine. Don't be afraid to revise and refine your twist until it has the impact you're looking for.

Common misconceptions about writing plot twists

Plot twists have to be shocking: While plot twists can certainly be shocking, they don't have to be. A good plot twist should be unexpected and surprising, but it doesn't necessarily have to be a "gotcha" moment.

Plot twists should come out of nowhere: A plot twist should be unexpected, but it shouldn't come completely out of nowhere. It's important to foreshadow the twist and lay the groundwork for it earlier in the story, even if it's in subtle ways.

All stories need a plot twist: Not every story needs a plot twist, and forcing one into a story where it doesn't fit can feel contrived. It's more important to focus on telling a compelling story with well-developed characters.

The plot twist is the most important part of the story: While a good plot twist can certainly be a memorable and impactful moment, it's not the only important part of the story. Characters, themes, and the overall story arc are all just as important.

Once the plot twist is revealed, the story is over: A plot twist should have consequences that ripple through the rest of the story. After the twist is revealed, there should still be story left to tell, as the characters deal with the aftermath of the twist.

Three famous plot twists

The Sixth Sense (1999), where it is revealed at the end of the movie that the main character, played by Bruce Willis, has been dead the entire time.

The Usual Suspects (1995), where the audience learns at the end of the movie that the supposed protagonist, played by Kevin Spacey, is actually the villain.

Psycho (1960), where it is revealed halfway through the movie that the supposed main character, played by Janet Leigh, is killed off, and the real main character is her killer, played by Anthony Perkins.

23

Red Herrings

Red herrings are a popular storytelling technique used in various genres, including romance novels.

They are essentially false clues that are introduced to distract the reader from the true outcome of the story.

Below are some common techniques used to introduce red herrings in a novel, as well as how they can be used effectively to create suspense and tension in a story, and some common mistakes writers make when using them.

Common techniques used to introduce red herrings:

One common technique is to introduce a suspicious character who seems to have motive or opportunity to commit the crime or create a problem in the romance novel.

The character may be seen doing something that looks suspicious, such as lurking around the scene of the crime or acting suspiciously in some other way. For example, in a romance novel, a jealous ex-lover may be introduced as a potential threat to the main couple's happiness, causing the reader to suspect them as the antagonist.

Another common technique is to create a situation that looks like it will be a significant problem for the main characters, but ultimately turns out to be a red herring. For example, a couple may have a serious disagreement that seems like it will lead to the end of their relationship, but it is later revealed to be a misunderstanding or miscommunication that is easily resolved.

How red herrings can be used effectively to create suspense and tension in a story:

Red herrings are a useful tool for building suspense and tension in a romance novel. They keep the reader guessing and create a sense of uncertainty about the outcome of the story. By introducing false clues and misdirection, the writer can build anticipation and heighten the stakes for the main characters. This can lead to a more immersive and engaging reading experience for the audience.

Certain genres that are better suited to the use of red herrings than others.

While red herrings can be used in any genre, they are most commonly associated with mystery and thriller novels.

However, they can be used effectively in romance novels as well. In fact, a well-placed red herring can be a great way to keep the reader engaged and invested in the romantic storyline.

How many red herrings is too many in a novel, and how to strike the right balance?

There is no hard and fast rule for the number of red herrings that should be used in a novel.

Too many red herrings can be overwhelming for the reader and make the story feel convoluted. On the other hand, too few red herrings can make the story predictable and unexciting. The key is to strike the right balance by introducing enough red herrings to keep the reader guessing, without overwhelming them with too many false clues.

How red herrings can be used as a way to misdirect readers from the true culprit in a mystery novel:

Red herrings can be used effectively to misdirect readers from the true culprit in a mystery novel. By introducing false clues and misdirection, the writer can build anticipation and heighten the stakes for the main characters. This can lead to a more immersive and engaging reading experience for the audience.

Common mistakes writers make when using red herrings, and how they can be avoided:

One common mistake writers make when using red herrings is introducing false clues that don't fit logically into the storyline. This can make the story feel contrived and unconvincing. Another mistake is introducing red herrings too early in the story, which can give the reader too much time to figure out what's really going on.

To avoid these mistakes, writers should ensure that their red herrings fit seamlessly into the story and are introduced at the right time.

How red herrings can be used to create character development and reveal hidden motivations:

Red herrings can be used effectively to reveal hidden motivations and create character development. By introducing false clues that lead the reader to suspect a particular character, the writer can use this as an opportunity to delve deeper into that character's motivations and backstory.

This can help to create a more complex and nuanced portrayal of the character, adding depth and dimension to the story.

Can red herrings be used in non-mystery genres to keep readers engaged and guessing?

While red herrings are commonly associated with mystery and thriller genres, they can be used in any genre to keep readers engaged and guessing. In a romance novel, for example, red herrings can be used to create uncertainty and tension in the relationship between the main characters.

By introducing obstacles or misunderstandings that seem insurmountable, the writer can keep the reader invested in the outcome of the story.

How do readers typically react to red herrings, and what impact can they have on the overall reading experience?

Readers generally enjoy red herrings, as they add an element of unpredictability and excitement to the story. When used effectively, red herrings can create a sense of anticipation and suspense that keeps the reader engaged and invested in the outcome of the story. However, if overused or poorly executed, red herrings can frustrate the reader and make the story feel contrived.

Are there any classic novels or authors that are particularly skilled at using red herrings, and what can we learn from their techniques?

Agatha Christie is a classic author who is known for her skilful use of red herrings in mystery novels. In her novel **"And Then There Were None,"** she introduces multiple red herrings to mislead the reader and keep them guessing about the true culprit. Her techniques included creating a diverse cast of characters with various motives and opportunities, as well as introducing false clues that seemed plausible but ultimately led nowhere. By studying her work, writers can learn how to effectively use red herrings to create suspense and intrigue in their own stories.

Your red herring checklist

If you're a beginner author looking to incorporate red herrings into your romance novel, here are some steps you can follow:

1. Identify the key moments of conflict in your romance novel.

This could be anything from a misunderstanding between the main characters to an external threat to their relationship.

2. Consider what characters, situations, or events could be introduced as red herrings to mislead the reader about the true outcome of the story.

For example, you might introduce a third character who seems to have a romantic interest in one of the main characters, causing the reader to question the outcome of the story.

3. Make sure that the red herrings you introduce fit logically into the storyline and don't feel contrived or forced.

They should be plausible enough to make the reader question the true outcome of the story.

4. Think about the pacing of your story and where the red herrings should be introduced.

You want to keep the reader guessing, but you also don't want to introduce too many false clues too early on in the story. A good rule of thumb is to introduce one or two key red herrings at the midpoint of the novel and then ramp up the tension from there.

5. Consider how the red herrings can be used to create character development and reveal hidden motivations.

By using false clues to misdirect the reader, you can create opportunities to delve deeper into the motivations and backstory of your characters.

6. Test your red herrings on beta readers or critique partners to get feedback on how effective they are in creating suspense and intrigue.

Use their feedback to fine-tune your red herrings and strike the right balance between keeping the reader guessing and overwhelming them with false clues.

By following these steps, you can effectively incorporate red herrings into your romance novel and create a more engaging and immersive reading experience for your audience.

24

Using Descriptive Language

How can I effectively use descriptive language to create vivid, engaging characters and settings in my romance novels?

To create vivid and engaging characters and settings in your romance novels, it is important to use descriptive language that is both specific and imaginative. When describing characters, think beyond their physical appearance and try to convey their personalities, quirks, and inner thoughts using vivid language. For example, instead of simply describing a character as *"attractive,"* you might say that their *"smoky eyes sparkled with a mischievous glint"* or that their *"gruff voice betrayed a hidden softness."*

To describe settings, use sensory details to create a sensory-rich environment that immerses your readers in the scene.

For example, you might describe the *"sun-dappled cobblestone streets"* of a quaint European village or the *"salty sea breeze"* of a beachside getaway.

What are some techniques for balancing descriptive language with action and plot progression in my writing?

When using descriptive language in your writing, it is important to strike a balance between describing the setting and characters and moving the plot forward. One technique for balancing these elements is to use descriptive language to enhance the action and plot progression.

For example, instead of simply describing a character walking through a park, you might use sensory details to create a more immersive scene. You could describe the *"crunch of leaves underfoot"* or the *"sharp scent of pine needles,"* which not only enhances the setting but also adds to the character's emotional state or the tension of the scene.

How can I use sensory details like smells, sounds, and textures to enhance the romantic atmosphere of my scenes?

Sensory details are a powerful tool for creating an immersive and romantic atmosphere in your scenes. When using sensory details, aim to describe the smells, sounds, and textures that evoke a sense of intimacy and closeness. For example, the *"sweet aroma of roses"* can evoke a sense of romance, while the *"gentle rustle of silk sheets"* can create an atmosphere of sensuality.

These details can be used to enhance the romantic connection between characters, creating a deeper sense of intimacy and emotion.

What are some common mistakes to avoid when using descriptive language in my romance writing?

One common mistake to avoid when using descriptive language in your romance writing is overusing adjectives or relying on cliches.

Instead, aim to use specific and imaginative language that creates a clear image in the reader's mind.

Another mistake is using too much description, which can slow down the pace of your story and distract from the plot. It's important to strike a balance between descriptive language and plot progression, so that your writing flows seamlessly and keeps the reader engaged.

How can I use descriptive language to create tension and anticipation in my romantic storylines?

Descriptive language can be used to create tension and anticipation in your romantic storylines by building a sense of anticipation or foreshadowing. For example, you might describe the *"dark clouds gathering on the horizon,"* or the *"quickening beat of her heart"* to create a sense of impending conflict or excitement.

You can also use descriptive language to create emotional tension between characters, highlighting the unspoken feelings that add complexity and depth to your story.

How do I strike a balance between using too much and too little descriptive language in my romance novels?

To strike a balance between using too much and too little descriptive language, aim to use description that is specific and relevant to the plot and characters. Use sensory details to create a sensory-rich environment, and be sure to vary the pace of your description so that it flows seamlessly with the plot. You should also consider the reader's attention span and avoid using unnecessary details that distract from the plot.

What are some effective ways to convey the setting of a romantic scene using descriptive language?

To effectively convey the setting of a romantic scene using descriptive language, use sensory details to create a vivid picture in the reader's mind. Focus on the details that evoke a sense of romance, such as lighting, scents, and sounds.

For example, you might describe the *"soft glow of candlelight"* in a dimly lit restaurant, or the *"crash of waves against the shore"* on a secluded beach. Be sure to incorporate the setting in a way that enhances the romantic connection between characters, and consider how the setting can be used to create conflict or tension in your plot.

How can I use descriptive language to create unique, memorable love interest characters in my romance novels?

To create unique, memorable love interest characters in your romance novels, use descriptive language that conveys their personalities, quirks, and unique traits. Consider their physical appearance and how it reflects their character, as well as their dialogue and actions.

For example, you might describe a character's *"crooked smile"* or the *"playful lilt in their voice."* Use sensory details to convey their emotions and create a sense of intimacy between them and the main character.

What are some tips for evoking strong emotions in readers using descriptive language, such as empathy or desire?

To evoke strong emotions in readers using descriptive language, use language that creates a visceral and emotional response. For example, you might use sensory details to create a sense of empathy, such as the *"wince of pain"* or the *"sinking feeling in the pit of her stomach."*

To create a sense of desire, use language that conveys passion and intimacy, such as the *"electricity in the air"* or the *"gentle brush of their fingertips."* Use descriptive language to convey a character's emotional state and to create a sense of empathy and connection between the reader and the characters.

How can I use descriptive language to create a particular mood or atmosphere in my romance novel, and what impact will it have on the overall tone of my writing?

To create a particular mood or atmosphere in your romance novel, use descriptive language that reflects the mood and tone of your story. For example, if you want to create a dreamy, romantic atmosphere, you might use language that evokes a sense of lightness and happiness, such as *"fluttering heartbeats"* or *"butterflies in the stomach."*

If you want to create a more intense, passionate atmosphere, you might use language that conveys urgency and desire, such as *"breathless anticipation"* or *"heart-pounding passion."*

The impact of descriptive language on the overall tone of your writing will be to create a more immersive and emotional reading experience for your readers.

Some unique examples you could use in your romance novel

"Her eyes were a deep, rich brown, warm and inviting."

"He had a way of making her feel like the only person in the room, with a smile that brightened her day."

"The air was heavy with the scent of roses, sweet and heady."

"She wore a dress that flowed like water, the fabric shimmering in the light."

"His touch was like fire, igniting a spark that she couldn't ignore."

"The sun shone down on them like a warm embrace, making them feel alive and free."

"She had a voice that was like honey, smooth and soothing."

"The sound of his laughter was infectious, making her own heart swell with happiness."

"The sky was a vibrant shade of blue, like the ocean on a clear day."

"His cologne was like a drug, intoxicating and alluring."

"Her hair was like spun gold, falling in soft waves around her face."

"The sound of rain tapping against the window was a comforting lullaby, soothing her to sleep."

"He had a way of looking at her that made her heart skip a beat, like she was the most beautiful thing he had ever seen."

"The room was bathed in the soft glow of candlelight, creating a romantic and intimate atmosphere."

"The texture of the sand between their toes was soft and grainy, a tangible reminder of the beauty of the moment."

"The moon cast a silvery glow over everything, creating a sense of magic and wonder."

"Her smile was like sunshine on a cloudy day, brightening everything around her."

"The sound of the waves lapping against the shore was a constant reminder of the peace and serenity of the moment."

"He had a way of touching her that was both gentle and passionate, a perfect blend of tenderness and desire."

"The breeze carried the scent of fresh-cut grass, a reminder of the simple joys of life."

How to actually create descriptive language like this

Creating descriptive language requires imagination, creativity, and attention to detail. Here are some techniques that can help you create vivid and engaging descriptions:

Use specific language: Instead of using general descriptions, be specific with your language to create a clear picture in the reader's mind. For example, instead of describing a character as *"beautiful,"* describe the shape of their eyes or the colour of their hair.

Incorporate sensory details: Sensory details, like smells, sounds, and textures, can make your descriptions more immersive and engaging. Consider how the scene or character would be experienced with all five senses, and try to incorporate those details in your writing.

Use metaphors and similes: Metaphors and similes can create interesting and imaginative descriptions that convey a deeper meaning. For example, describing someone's smile as *"bright as the sun"* or a character's voice as *"smooth as silk."*

Vary the pace: Vary the pace of your descriptions to match the mood and tone of the scene. For example, use short, choppy sentences to create tension and suspense, or longer, flowing sentences to convey a sense of relaxation or romance.

Avoid clichés: Clichés are overused and unoriginal descriptions that can detract from the impact of your writing. Instead, aim to create fresh, unique descriptions that will engage and surprise your reader.

Consider the character's perspective: Descriptions should be influenced by the character's perspective and emotional state. Consider how the character would experience the scene or setting, and use language that reflects their mood and personality.

The 5 senses

Using all five senses to create descriptive language in a romance novel can help the reader experience the scene more vividly and create a deeper emotional connection to the characters.

Here are some examples of how to use each sense to create descriptive language:

Sight: Use descriptive language to paint a visual picture for the reader. For example, *"The sun sank below the horizon, painting the sky with hues of pink and orange. Shadows grew long, and the world was bathed in a warm, golden light."*

Hearing: Use descriptive language to convey the sounds of the scene or the character's voice. For example, *"The waves crashed against the shore, the sound like a soothing lullaby. His voice was deep and rich, like velvet against her skin."*

Smell: Use descriptive language to create a sense of atmosphere or to convey the scent of a character or scene. For example, *"The air was heavy with the scent of roses, sweet and heady. He smelled like fresh pine, a scent that reminded her of home."*

Taste: Use descriptive language to convey the taste of food or drink, or to describe a character's lips or kiss. For example, *"The wine* *was rich and full-bodied, with notes of blackberry and vanilla. His lips were warm and tasted of mint, sending shivers down her spine."*

Touch: Use descriptive language to convey the texture of objects or the feeling of touch between characters. For example, *"The sand was soft and grainy, slipping through her fingers like silk. His touch was gentle but electric, sending tingles down her spine."*

By incorporating all five senses into your writing, you can create a more immersive and engaging experience for the reader. It can also help to create a sense of intimacy and emotional connection between the characters and the reader.

25

Writing Dialogue In Your Romance Novel

How do I make my dialogue sound realistic and authentic in my romance novel?

To make your dialogue sound realistic and authentic, try to write it the way people actually talk. Use contractions and sentence fragments, and avoid overly formal or flowery language. Pay attention to the rhythm of speech and the use of pauses and interruptions, and use those to create a more natural flow to your dialogue.

Here's an example of how to make your dialogue sound realistic and authentic in a romance novel:

Instead of writing:

"I cannot believe you would do such a thing," said Jane indignantly.

Write:

"I can't believe you'd do something like that," Jane said, her voice tense with anger. "How could you?"

In this example, Jane's dialogue sounds more realistic because it uses contractions and sentence fragments, which is how people naturally talk in everyday conversation.

The use of pauses and interruptions also helps create a more natural flow to the dialogue, making it sound more authentic. Additionally, the use of descriptive language, such as *"her voice tense with anger,"* adds to the realism of the dialogue by conveying the character's emotions and helping to bring the scene to life.

How can I use dialogue to develop my characters in my romance novel?

Dialogue is a powerful tool for developing your characters in a romance novel. Use it to reveal their personalities, quirks, and unique traits. Consider how each character would speak and the language they would use. Use dialogue to convey their emotions, and to reveal their fears and desires. Use it to show their strengths and weaknesses, and to create conflict or tension in your plot.

Here's an example of how to use dialogue to develop characters in a romance novel:

Instead of writing:

Mary was a strong and independent woman who didn't like to take orders from anyone.

Write:

"I'm sorry, I can't just sit back and let you do this," Mary said firmly. "I need to take care of myself and make my own decisions."

In this example, Mary's dialogue reveals her personality and character traits by showing that she is assertive and values her independence. Her language and tone are reflective of her strength and confidence. By using dialogue to reveal these traits, the character is developed in a way that is more engaging and realistic for the reader.

Additionally, the dialogue helps to advance the plot and create tension by introducing a conflict between Mary and another character who may not share her values

How can I use dialogue to create chemistry between my characters in my romance novel?

Dialogue is a key way to create chemistry between your characters in a romance novel. Use it to create banter and playful teasing, and to reveal their mutual attraction. Use it to create a sense of intimacy between them, and to show their emotional connection. Use dialogue to create conflict or misunderstandings that create tension and add to the overall romantic arc.

Here's an example of how to use dialogue to create chemistry between characters in a romance novel:

Instead of writing:

"Hi," said John.
"Hello," replied Jane.

Write:

"Hey there, beautiful," John said with a smile.

Jane blushed. "Stop it, you're making me nervous," she said, giggling.

In this example, the dialogue between John and Jane creates chemistry by showing their playful banter and mutual attraction. John's use of a playful and flirtatious nickname creates an immediate sense of intimacy and attraction between the characters. Jane's response, blushing and giggling, reveals her own attraction and creates a sense of mutual interest.

The dialogue also creates a sense of tension and anticipation, as the reader wonders if the characters will act on their attraction or if there will be further misunderstandings or conflicts between them. By using dialogue to create chemistry between characters, the reader is drawn deeper into the romantic arc of the story.

How do I balance dialogue with narrative in my romance novel?

To balance dialogue with narrative in your romance novel, use dialogue to move the story forward and reveal important information about your characters. Use narrative to set the scene, describe the action, and convey the character's internal thoughts and feelings. Vary the length and frequency of your dialogue to match the mood and tone of the scene.

Here's an example of how to balance dialogue with narrative in a romance novel:

Instead of writing:

John and Jane sat down at the restaurant. They looked at the menu and then ordered their food. They chatted while they waited for their meals to arrive.

Write:

John and Jane sat down at the cosy Italian restaurant, the aroma of garlic and tomatoes wafting through the air. They looked over the menu, taking their time to decide on the perfect meal.

"I've heard the pasta here is amazing," Jane said, smiling at John.

John chuckled. "Then that's what we'll have," he said, his eyes sparkling.

As they waited for their meals to arrive, they chatted about their day and their plans for the future.

In this example, the narrative description sets the scene and creates a sense of atmosphere, while the dialogue reveals information about the characters and advances the plot.

The use of sensory details, such as the smell of the food, creates a richer and more immersive experience for the reader. The dialogue is used to create chemistry between the characters, revealing their shared interests and sense of humour. By varying the length and frequency of the dialogue, the scene has a natural and engaging flow that helps to balance the dialogue with the narrative description.

How do I write effective subtext in my dialogue for my romance novel?

Subtext is the underlying message or meaning conveyed in a character's dialogue. To write effective subtext in your romance novel, consider the character's emotional state and what they are not saying. Use body language and nonverbal cues to convey their true feelings, and use dialogue that reveals their true intentions. Use subtext to create tension and conflict in your story.

Here's an example of how to write effective subtext in dialogue for a romance novel:

Instead of writing:

"I'm fine," Mary said with a smile.

Write:

Mary forced a smile, trying to hide the sadness in her eyes. "I'm fine," she said, her voice tight.

In this example, Mary's dialogue has a hidden subtext that reveals her true emotional state. Her forced smile and tight voice show that she is not fine, even though she says she is.

By using subtext in this way, the reader is drawn deeper into the character's emotional journey, and the tension is increased. Subtext can also be used to create conflict or tension between characters by revealing that their true intentions are not aligned. For example, one character may say one thing, while their subtext reveals something entirely different, creating misunderstandings and conflict that drive the story forward.

How do I use dialogue to move the plot forward in my romance novel?

Dialogue is a powerful way to move the plot forward in a romance novel. Use it to reveal important information and to create conflict or tension. Use dialogue to show the characters' reactions to events in the story, and to advance the overall romantic arc.

Here's an example of how to use dialogue to move the plot forward in a romance novel:

Instead of writing:

Jane arrived at the party and saw John across the room. She walked over to him and they started chatting.

Write:

Jane's heart raced as she scanned the crowded party for a familiar face. Finally, her eyes settled on John, looking as handsome as ever across the room.

"Hey there," she said, her voice a little too high-pitched.
"Jane, hi!" John said, grinning. "I'm so glad you made it."

As they chatted, Jane couldn't help but notice the way John's eyes kept darting nervously towards the entrance. It wasn't until she heard a commotion that she realised what was happening - her ex-boyfriend had just arrived, and he was making a scene.

In this example, the dialogue is used to reveal important information that moves the plot forward. The use of descriptive language, such as Jane's racing heart, adds to the tension and creates a sense of anticipation for the reader. The dialogue between Jane and John advances the plot by setting up the conflict that will drive the story forward.

By showing the characters' reactions to events in the story, the reader is drawn deeper into the narrative and invested in the outcome.

How do I use pacing to create tension in my dialogue in my romance novel?

Pacing is the speed at which your dialogue unfolds. To create tension in your dialogue, vary the pace to match the emotional state of your characters. Use short, choppy sentences to create a sense of urgency or excitement, and longer, flowing sentences to create a sense of intimacy or tenderness. Use pauses and silences to create a sense of tension or conflict.

Here's an example of how to use pacing to create tension in dialogue in a romance novel:

Instead of writing:

"I don't know if I'm ready for this," John said, nervously.
"Don't worry, it'll be fine," Jane said, reassuringly.

Write:

"I don't know if I'm ready for this," John said, his voice trembling.

"You have to be," Jane said, her words firm and unwavering. "This is what we've been working towards all these months. We can't turn back now."

John looked at Jane, his eyes searching hers for some sign of doubt. When he found none, he took a deep breath and nodded. "You're right," he said, his voice steadier. "Let's do this."

In this example, the pacing of the dialogue is used to create tension and a sense of urgency. John's short, trembling sentence adds to the tension and creates a sense of anticipation for the reader. Jane's longer, flowing sentence provides a counterpoint to John's anxious energy, creating a sense of balance and stability.

The use of pauses and silences, such as when John searches Jane's eyes for reassurance, adds to the tension and helps to create a more immersive experience for the reader. By using pacing to create tension in dialogue, the story becomes more engaging and emotionally impactful for the reader.

How can I use dialogue to create a sense of setting in my romance novel?

Dialogue can be used to create a sense of setting in your romance novel. Use dialogue that reflects the culture or geography of the setting, and use it to reveal the character's relationship to the setting. For example, in a novel set in a beach town, you might use dialogue that references the ocean, the sand, or the local beachfront restaurants.

Here's an example of how to use dialogue to create a sense of setting in a romance novel:

Instead of writing:

Jane walked down the street towards the beach. She saw the waves crashing against the shore and felt the sand between her toes.

Write:

"Wow, the ocean is really something," Jane said, taking in the view.

John grinned. "You're telling me. I've lived here my whole life and I still can't get enough of it."

As they walked along the beach, Jane noticed the smell of saltwater and sunscreen in the air. "What's that restaurant over there?" she asked, nodding towards a beachfront patio.

"That's The Crab Shack. They have the best seafood in town," John said, pointing towards the restaurant.

In this example, the dialogue is used to create a sense of setting by referencing the ocean, the sand, and the local beachfront restaurants. The characters' dialogue reflects the culture and geography of the setting, and helps to create a more immersive experience for the reader.

The use of descriptive language, such as the smell of saltwater and sunscreen, adds to the sense of place and helps to make the setting feel more real. By using dialogue to create a sense of setting, the reader is drawn deeper into the story and invested in the characters' journey.

How can I use dialogue to create a unique voice for my characters in my romance novel?

Creating a unique voice for each character is an important part of writing dialogue in a romance novel. To do this, consider the character's personality, background, and motivations. Use dialogue that reflects their unique perspective and use it to reveal their quirks and idiosyncrasies. Use the character's voice to create conflict or tension in your story.

Here's an example of how to use dialogue to create a unique voice for characters in a romance novel:

Instead of writing:

John and Jane had a conversation about their relationship.

Write:

"So, where do you see this going?" Jane asked, fidgeting with her hands.

John sighed, running a hand through his hair. "I don't know, Jane. I mean, I love you, but I feel like we're stuck in a rut."

"Well, what do you want to do?" Jane asked, her voice rising a little.

"I want to travel," John said, his eyes lighting up. "I want to see the world and experience new things. But it feels like we're always stuck in the same routine, and I just...I don't know."

In this example, the use of unique voices for John and Jane creates a more engaging and emotionally impactful scene. John's dialogue reveals his desire for adventure and his frustration with the status quo, while Jane's dialogue shows her anxiety and concern about their relationship. By using dialogue that reflects the characters' personalities and motivations, the reader is drawn deeper into their emotional journey and invested in the outcome.

The use of rising tension in Jane's voice, and the slight pause in John's speech, add to the tension and create a more immersive experience for the reader. By using dialogue to create unique voices for your characters, your romance novel becomes more engaging and emotionally resonant.

How can I avoid common dialogue pitfalls in my romance novel?

Common pitfalls to avoid in writing dialogue in a romance novel include overusing dialogue tags, using clichés, and creating unrealistic or stilted dialogue. To avoid these pitfalls, edit your dialogue carefully, and make sure that it sounds authentic and true to the characters.

How can I use dialogue to create conflict in my romance novel?

Dialogue is a powerful tool for creating conflict in a romance novel. Use it to reveal conflicting opinions, beliefs, or desires between characters. Use dialogue to create misunderstandings or miscommunications that lead to conflict or tension. Use dialogue to show the characters' emotional reactions to events in the story, and to create tension between them.

Here's an example of how to use dialogue to create conflict in a romance novel:

Instead of writing:

John and Jane had a conversation about where to go on vacation.

Write:

"I was thinking we could go to Paris this year," John said, grinning.

"Paris?" Jane's voice rose. "Are you kidding me? We can't afford to go to Paris. And what about your promise to take me to Hawaii?"

"I never promised that," John said, his smile fading. "And besides, I think it would be a great opportunity for us to see the world together."

Jane rolled her eyes. "I don't want to see the world. I want to relax on a beach and drink margaritas. You're always so focused on adventure and travel."

In this example, the dialogue is used to create conflict between John and Jane over where to go on vacation. Their differing opinions and desires are revealed through their dialogue, creating tension and conflict between them. The use of rising tension in Jane's voice and the fading of John's smile adds to the sense of conflict and creates a more immersive experience for the reader.

By using dialogue to create conflict in your romance novel, your characters become more complex and their relationships become more emotionally resonant.

How can I use dialogue to reveal information in my romance novel without being too obvious?

To reveal information without being too obvious, use dialogue that is subtle and nuanced. Avoid heavy-handed exposition, and instead, use dialogue that conveys information indirectly. Use dialogue that reveals a character's motivations or emotions, and use it to create subtext that reveals important information.

Here's an example of how to use dialogue to reveal information in a subtle way in a romance novel:

Instead of writing:

"Can you believe it's been six months since we started dating?" John said.

"I know, time flies when you're having fun," Jane replied.

"I have something I want to ask you," John said, getting down on one knee. "Will you marry me?"

"Yes!" Jane cried, throwing her arms around him.

Write:

John and Jane sat on the couch, watching the sunset over the beach.

"Remember when we first met here?" John said, his voice soft.

Jane smiled, remembering the day vividly. "How could I forget?"

"I knew from that first day that you were the one," John said, taking her hand. "I love you more every day, and I can't imagine my life without you."

Jane felt her heart race at his words, and a tear slipped down her cheek. "I love you too," she whispered.

In this example, the information that John is going to propose to Jane is revealed through his words and actions, but not directly stated. The use of descriptive language and subtext helps to create a more subtle and nuanced reveal, which can make the moment more emotionally impactful for the reader.

By using dialogue to reveal information in a subtle way, you can create a more engaging and emotionally resonant romance novel.

How do I create a balance between dialogue and action in my romance novel?

To create a balance between dialogue and action in your romance novel, use dialogue to move the story forward and to reveal important information about your characters. Use action to create tension and to advance the plot. Vary the length and frequency of your dialogue to match the mood and tone of the scene.

Here's an example of how to create a balance between dialogue and action in a romance novel:

Instead of writing:

John and Jane had a long conversation about their relationship.

They discussed their hopes, fears, and dreams, and the conversation became emotional and intense.

Write:

John and Jane stood on the beach, the wind blowing through their hair.

"I love you," John said, taking Jane's hand. "But we need to talk about our future."

Jane's heart sank at his words. "What do you mean?"

"I mean that I want more," *John said, his voice steady.* "I want to move in together, and eventually get married. But I don't want to pressure you into anything."

Jane felt a lump form in her throat. She loved John, but the thought of moving in together terrified her. "I don't know if I'm ready for that," *she said, her voice shaking.*

John nodded, his eyes filled with understanding. "I just want you to know how I feel. I don't want to push you into anything, but I need to be honest about what I want."

In this example, the use of action and dialogue are balanced to create a scene that is emotionally resonant and moves the story forward. The dialogue is used to reveal the characters' emotions and desires, while the action is used to create tension and to advance the plot.

By using a balance of dialogue and action in your romance novel, you can create a more engaging and immersive experience for the reader.

How can I use dialogue to create an emotional impact in my romance novel?

Dialogue is a powerful way to create an emotional impact in a romance novel. Use it to convey the character's emotions, and to show their vulnerability and desires. Use dialogue to reveal the character's internal conflicts and to create a sense of empathy in the reader. Use dialogue to create an emotional connection between the characters and the reader.

Here's an example of how to use dialogue to create an emotional impact in a romance novel:

Instead of writing:

John and Jane had an emotional conversation about their relationship.

They both cried and hugged each other, and the conversation ended on a positive note.

Write:

John and Jane sat on the couch, their eyes locked in a deep gaze.

"I'm scared," Jane whispered, her voice trembling.

John took her hand, his eyes filled with concern. "Scared of what?"

"Of losing you," Jane said, tears welling up in her eyes. "I don't know what I'd do without you."

John felt his heart ache at her words. He had no idea that Jane felt this way. "I'm not going anywhere," he said, pulling her into a tight embrace. "I love you, and I'll always be here for you."

Jane buried her face in his chest, feeling a wave of relief wash over her. "I love you too," she said, her voice muffled.

In this example, the dialogue is used to create an emotional impact by revealing the character's fears and vulnerabilities. The use of descriptive language and actions also helps to create a more immersive and emotionally resonant scene.

By using dialogue to reveal the characters' emotions and vulnerabilities, you can create a deeper emotional connection between the characters and the reader, and make your romance novel more engaging and impactful.

26

How To End Your Novel

There are many different types of endings for a romance novel, and the best type of ending will depend on the specific story and characters. Here are some examples of common types of endings for a romance novel:

Happily ever after (HEA): The most classic and popular ending for a romance novel is the HEA ending, where the main characters end up together and in love. This is a satisfying and emotionally resonant ending for readers who want a feel-good story. An example of an HEA ending is the end of **"Pride and Prejudice"** by Jane Austen, where Elizabeth and Darcy confess their love for each other and get married.

Happy for now (HFN): A variation on the HEA ending is the HFN ending, where the characters may not end up together forever, but they are happy and in love for now. This type of ending is useful for stories where the characters have more obstacles to overcome or where the author wants to leave room for a possible sequel. An example of an HFN ending is the end of **"The Fault in Our Stars"** by John Green, where Hazel and Augustus are happy together but Augustus is dying of cancer.

Bittersweet: A bittersweet ending is one where the characters do not end up together, but they have learned something valuable about themselves and have grown as individuals. This type of ending is useful for stories where the focus is on character development rather than a happy ending. An example of a bittersweet ending is the end of **"Gone with the Wind"** by Margaret Mitchell, where Rhett and Scarlett do not end up together, but Scarlett realises that she loves him and will always love him.

Tragic: A tragic ending is one where one or both of the main characters dies or experiences a terrible loss. This type of ending is useful for stories where the focus is on the harsh realities of life and the consequences of the characters' actions. An example of a tragic ending is the end of **"Romeo and Juliet"** by William Shakespeare, where Romeo and Juliet both die.

Open-ended: An open-ended ending is one where the story does not have a clear resolution, and the reader is left to imagine what might happen next. This type of ending is useful for stories where the focus is on the journey rather than the destination. An example of an open-ended ending is the end of **"The Great Gatsby"** by F. Scott Fitzgerald, where the reader is left to wonder what will happen to Nick and the other characters in the future.

These are just a few examples of the different types of endings for a romance novel, and there are many other variations and combinations of these types. The best type of ending for a story will depend on the characters, the plot, and the author's goals for the story.

How to create an amazing ending for your romance novel

Creating an amazing ending for your romance novel can be a challenging and rewarding experience. Here are some tips to help you create an ending that will leave your readers satisfied and emotionally moved:

Stay true to the story: The ending of your romance novel should feel authentic and true to the story you've told. Make sure the resolution fits the characters and the plot you've developed. Don't try to force a particular type of ending just because it's popular or expected.

Create emotional impact: Your ending should be emotionally resonant for your readers. This means creating a scene that pulls at the heartstrings and leaves a lasting impression. Use dialogue, description, and action to create a sense of emotional closure for your characters and your readers.

Provide a sense of resolution: The ending of your romance novel should provide a sense of resolution for your characters and your readers. This doesn't necessarily mean a happily-ever-after ending, but it does mean providing closure and a sense of completion for the story you've told. Make sure loose ends are tied up and questions are answered.

Use symbolism: Symbolism can be a powerful tool in creating an amazing ending for your romance novel. Use recurring images or motifs from throughout the story to create a sense of deeper meaning and resonance. For example, if your story features a recurring image of roses, you might use this image to create a sense of finality and closure in your ending.

Consider your readers: Your ending should be satisfying for your readers. Think about the emotional journey you've taken them on and what they'll be looking for in a resolution. Make sure your ending is emotionally satisfying and leaves a positive impression.

Don't be afraid to take risks: A truly amazing ending might involve taking risks or subverting reader expectations. If you have an unconventional ending in mind that fits the story, don't be afraid to try it. Sometimes the most memorable and powerful endings are the ones that break the mould.

Overall, creating an amazing ending for your romance novel requires careful consideration of the story, characters, and reader expectations. Stay true to the story and emotional impact you want to create, and use all the tools at your disposal to craft an ending that will leave your readers satisfied and moved.

How do I ensure that my ending is emotionally satisfying?

Your ending should provide closure for the story you've told and leave readers feeling emotionally moved. Consider the emotional journey you've taken readers on and use dialogue, action, and description to create a sense of finality.

Should I always go for a happy ending in my romance novel?

Not necessarily. While many romance novels end with a happy ending, it's important to stay true to the story you're telling. Don't be afraid to create an ending that fits the characters and plot, even if it's not what readers expect.

How do I create a sense of resolution without tying up every loose end?

The ending of your romance novel should provide a sense of closure and resolution, but it doesn't need to answer every question or resolve every plot thread. Instead, focus on creating an emotional resolution that feels true to the story you've told.

How do I create an ending that readers will remember?

A memorable ending is one that leaves readers emotionally moved and resonant. Consider using symbolism, powerful dialogue, or a surprising twist to create a sense of lasting impact.

How do I avoid clichés in my romance novel ending?

Clichés are overused and predictable, so it's important to avoid them in your ending. Consider the unique elements of your story and characters, and use those to create an ending that feels fresh and original.

How do I ensure that my ending is true to my characters?

Your characters should feel authentic and true to themselves in the ending of your romance novel. Consider their emotional journeys and motivations, and make sure the resolution feels true to their growth and development.

Should I tie up all loose ends in my romance novel ending?

While it's important to provide a sense of resolution in your ending, it's not necessary to tie up every loose end. Leave some things to the imagination of the reader, and focus on creating an emotional resolution instead.

How do I create a sense of finality without feeling rushed?

The ending of your romance novel should feel final and satisfying, but not rushed. Take your time in building up to the resolution, using dialogue, action, and description to create a sense of emotional closure.

How do I balance a satisfying ending with a realistic one?

While a satisfying ending is important, it's also important to stay true to the characters and story you've told. Consider the real-life implications of the events of your story, and use that to create an ending that feels both satisfying and realistic.

Endings - What your readers hate

Romance readers are generally looking for an emotionally satisfying ending that provides a sense of closure to the story they've invested in. However, there are a few common things that romance readers may dislike about endings:

Cliffhangers: Readers generally prefer a complete resolution to the story they've invested in, and cliffhangers that leave major questions unanswered can be frustrating.

To avoid leaving major questions unanswered and frustrating readers with a cliffhanger, you should take the following steps:

Plan the ending in advance: As you write your novel, think about the ending you want to create. Decide what questions need to be answered and how you will tie up the loose ends. This will help you avoid accidentally leaving a cliffhanger.

We recommend you check out our *'How To Write a Winning Novel Outline – Romance Workbook'*)

Wrap up subplots: Make sure you've resolved all of the subplots in your story, not just the main romance plot. This will provide a sense of closure to your readers and help avoid any lingering questions.

Use foreshadowing: Throughout the story, hint at what's to come in the ending. This can help prepare readers for the resolution and avoid any unexpected surprises.

Avoid overly ambiguous endings: While a little ambiguity can be effective, be careful not to leave things too open-ended. Your readers have invested time and emotion into the story, and they will appreciate a satisfying resolution.

Test your ending with beta readers: Before finalising your ending, have beta readers read your manuscript and provide feedback. This can help you identify any potential cliffhangers or unanswered questions and make necessary revisions.

By taking these steps, you can create an ending that provides a complete resolution to the story and avoids frustrating readers with cliffhangers.

Unearned happy endings: While happy endings are a common feature of romance novels, readers may feel let down if the ending feels contrived or unearned. The characters and plot should lead naturally to the ending, rather than feeling forced or unrealistic.

To avoid an unearned happy ending that feels contrived or unrealistic, you can take the following steps:

Develop realistic characters: Make sure your characters are fully fleshed out and have believable motivations and backstories. Their actions and decisions should feel natural and authentic.

Build up to the ending: The ending should be a culmination of the character's journey throughout the story. Make sure the story builds towards the ending and that it feels like a natural progression of events.

Create conflict and tension: The path to a happy ending should be difficult and fraught with conflict. Make sure the characters face real challenges and obstacles that they need to overcome to achieve their happy ending.

Avoid easy solutions: Don't rely on unrealistic coincidences or sudden changes of heart to resolve conflicts or bring characters together. This can feel contrived and unearned.

Be true to your story: Don't try to force a happy ending if it doesn't feel true to the story you've created. Sometimes, a bittersweet or ambiguous ending can be more emotionally satisfying than a happy ending that feels unearned.

By taking these steps, you can create a happy ending that feels authentic and well-earned, and avoids leaving readers feeling let down or unsatisfied.

Lack of closure: Similarly, readers may dislike an ending that leaves too many loose ends or unanswered questions. While it's not necessary to tie up every plot thread, the ending should provide a sense of resolution and emotional closure.

To avoid a lack of closure in your romance novel's ending, you can take the following steps:

Identify all loose ends: Make a list of all the unresolved questions or loose ends in your story. Determine which ones are important to the overall plot and character arcs, and which ones are less critical.

Tie up loose ends: For the important loose ends, make sure they are addressed in some way in the ending. This can be done through dialogue, action, or reflection by the characters.

Provide emotional closure: The ending should also provide emotional closure for the characters and the reader. Make sure the characters have achieved their goals or found a sense of peace or happiness. The reader should feel a sense of catharsis or satisfaction at the conclusion of the story.

Don't over-explain: While it's important to provide closure, be careful not to over-explain or tie up every loose end too neatly. Leave some room for the reader's imagination and interpretation.

Revisit earlier themes: Look back at earlier themes and motifs in the story and tie them in to the ending. This can provide a satisfying sense of completion and add resonance to the overall story.

By taking these steps, you can create an ending that ties up loose ends and provides emotional closure, without feeling too neat or over-explained.

Unrealistic plot twists: Plot twists can be effective in creating a memorable ending, but readers may dislike twists that feel unrealistic or contrived. The plot should feel authentic to the characters and story you've told.

To avoid unrealistic plot twists in your romance novel's ending, you can take the following steps:

Stay true to the story: The ending should feel authentic to the characters and plot you've established throughout the novel. Make sure any twists or surprises are rooted in the story you've told, and not forced or contrived.

Foreshadow: If you're planning a plot twist in the ending, make sure to foreshadow it earlier in the story. This can help it feel more organic and less like a gimmick.

Consider the characters: Plot twists should also feel authentic to the characters involved. Make sure the twist is consistent with their personalities, motivations, and past actions.

Don't rely on shock value: While plot twists can be effective, don't rely solely on shock value to create a memorable ending. The characters and their emotional journeys should still be the focus of the story.

Test it out: Consider getting feedback on the twist from beta readers or critique partners. This can help you gauge whether the twist feels authentic and satisfying to readers.

By taking these steps, you can create a plot twist that feels earned and authentic to the story and characters, while still providing a memorable ending for your romance novel.

Lack of emotional payoff: Ultimately, romance readers are invested in the emotional journey of the characters, and the ending should provide a sense of emotional payoff for the story they've invested in. A lack of emotional resonance can leave readers feeling unsatisfied with the ending.

To avoid a lack of emotional payoff in your romance novel's ending, you can take the following steps:

Stay true to the emotional journey: The ending should feel consistent with the emotional journey of the characters throughout the novel. Make sure the emotional resolution feels earned and not forced.

Deliver on the promises: If you've set up emotional stakes throughout the story, make sure to deliver on them in the ending. For example, if a character has been struggling with trust issues, make sure the ending shows them overcoming those issues in a meaningful way.

Show the characters' growth: The ending should show the characters' growth and how they've changed throughout the story. This can help readers feel invested in their emotional journey and satisfied with the ending.

Use sensory language: Use sensory language to convey the emotional impact of the ending. Use details like the character's body language, facial expressions, and tone of voice to show how they're feeling.

Avoid melodrama: While it's important to create a sense of emotional payoff, avoid melodrama and clichéd romance tropes. The ending should feel authentic and earned, not over-the-top or cheesy.

By taking these steps, you can create an ending that provides a satisfying emotional payoff for your readers and feels authentic to the story and characters you've created in your romance novel.

27

Romance Novel Book Titles

Creating a strong title for a romance novel is important as it can impact the book's sales and the interest of potential readers.

The audience for romance novels can vary, but typically includes women between the ages of 18 and 54.

A well-crafted title can capture the reader's attention and evoke a sense of the story's genre, mood, and themes.

There are several unusual ways and techniques that you can use to create a book title for your romance novel. Here are a few ideas:

Use a quote: Consider using a memorable quote from your novel as the title. This can be a great way to give readers a sense of what the book is about, while also piquing their curiosity.

Make a list: Create a list of words or phrases that are associated with your novel, such as character names, settings, themes, or plot points. Play around with different combinations and see what sounds interesting or intriguing.

Get inspiration from other media: Look to other forms of media, such as song lyrics, movie titles, or poetry, for inspiration. Try to find something that captures the essence of your book and will make readers curious to know more.

Use a metaphor: Consider using a metaphor that relates to your novel in some way. This can be a creative way to give readers a sense of what the book is about while also making the title memorable.

Create a pun: Puns can be a fun and memorable way to create a book title. Look for ways to play on words or use double meanings to create a title that is both clever and descriptive.

Try a question: A title that is phrased as a question can be an effective way to pique readers' curiosity and encourage them to pick up your book. Consider a question that relates to the central conflict or theme of your novel.

Use alliteration: Alliteration is the repetition of a consonant sound at the beginning of two or more words in a phrase. This can be a creative and memorable way to create a title that sticks in readers' minds.

Remember, your book title is an important part of your marketing strategy, and it's the first thing that readers will see. It should be descriptive, memorable, and give readers a sense of what they can expect from your book.

Here are some key considerations and steps for creating a compelling title for a romance novel:

Consider the genre and themes: The title should give readers a sense of the story's genre and themes. A title like **"Love in the Time of Cholera"** by Gabriel Garcia Marquez, for example, hints at the historical setting and the theme of enduring love. **"The Wedding Date"** by Jasmine

Guillory, on the other hand, indicates a contemporary romantic comedy.

Make it memorable: A memorable title can help the book stand out among the thousands of other romance novels on the market. A title like **"The Notebook"** by Nicholas Sparks, for example, is simple yet memorable and has become synonymous with the author's brand.

Keep it concise: Shorter titles tend to be more memorable and easier to remember. Consider titles like **"The Fault in Our Stars"** by John Green or **"Me Before You"** by Jojo Moyes.

Research the competition: Check out the titles of other popular romance novels in the same genre to get a sense of what works and what doesn't. Avoid titles that are too similar to other books, as this can lead to confusion among readers.

In summary, creating a strong title for a romance novel requires careful consideration of the genre, themes, and target audience. A memorable and concise title that accurately reflects the story can capture the reader's attention and lead to increased sales and interest.

What are the key elements of a good romance novel title?

A good romance novel title should be catchy, memorable, and give readers a sense of the story's tone, genre, and themes. It should also reflect the characters and their journey in some way.

How can I brainstorm ideas for my romance novel title?

Brainstorming ideas for your romance novel title can involve several techniques. You can start with a word or phrase that encapsulates the story's theme or tone, or think about catchy phrases or puns that tie into the plot. You can also consider using a quote from the novel or a phrase from a pivotal moment.

Should I use a specific formula when creating a romance novel title?

There is no one-size-fits-all formula for creating a romance novel title, but some popular techniques include using alliteration, wordplay, and catchy phrases that reflect the book's themes or characters.

How can I make sure my romance novel title stands out?

To make your title stand out, try to make it unique and memorable. Avoid clichés or overused phrases, and consider using unexpected or attention-grabbing word combinations.

Should my romance novel title be straightforward or mysterious?

The best title for your romance novel will depend on the story and its tone. Some titles are straightforward and descriptive, while others are more mysterious or ambiguous. Consider which approach best reflects the themes and characters in your story.

How can I make sure my romance novel title is marketable?

To make your romance novel title marketable, consider the genre and audience you're writing for. Look at other successful titles in the same genre and see what techniques they use. You can also do market research and test different title ideas with potential readers.

What are some common mistakes to avoid when creating a romance novel title?

Common mistakes to avoid include using titles that are too generic or vague, using cliché phrases or puns, or choosing a title that doesn't reflect the story or characters in a meaningful way.

How can I test my romance novel title before publishing?

To test your title, you can get feedback from beta readers, writer's groups, or social media followers. You can also do market research and see how potential readers respond to different title ideas.

How important is the cover art in conjunction with the book title?

The cover art is important in conjunction with the book title as it gives readers an initial impression of the story and sets expectations for the book. The title and cover art should work together to create a cohesive and attractive package.

28

Romance Writing Word Count

The word count for a romance novel can vary depending on the sub-genre, but a typical length is around **70,000 to 90,000** words.

To break this down into a daily word count target for 5 days a week, you could aim for around 1,400 to 1,800 words per writing session.

This would give you a total of around 7,000 to 9,000 words per week, which would allow you to complete a 70,000 to 90,000 word novel in about 10 to 13 weeks.

Of course, everyone's writing process is different, so you may find that you write more or less than this amount per session. The most important thing is to set a realistic goal that works for you and to be consistent in your writing practice.

29

Romance Fiction Book Cover Tips

A professional-looking book cover is incredibly important for a romance author for several reasons. First and foremost, it's the first thing a potential reader will see when browsing for a new book to read. If the cover doesn't catch their attention, they may never even read the blurb or consider purchasing the book. A poorly designed cover can also give the impression that the book is of low quality, which can negatively impact the author's reputation and future sales.

A professional-looking book cover can also help an author stand out in a crowded market. There are many romance novels out there, and a great cover can help your book stand out from the competition. A unique and visually striking cover can create interest and intrigue, and draw readers in who might not have otherwise considered your book.

Investing time and money into a professional-looking book cover can also lead to more positive reviews and increased sales. A well-designed cover can create a sense of professionalism and quality, and readers may be more likely to recommend the book to others if they feel it is of high quality.

Know your genre: Look at other successful book covers in the romance genre and take note of what design elements they have in common.

Choose an appropriate colour palette: The colours you choose should reflect the tone and mood of your story. Bold, bright colours work well for more light-hearted romance novels, while darker, more muted tones are better for serious or dramatic stories.

Use high-quality images: Choose images that are sharp and clear, and have a high resolution.

Avoid overused images: Avoid using cliché images like roses, hearts, or couples embracing. Instead, try to find a unique image that reflects the specific story you're telling.

Make the title legible: Choose a font that is easy to read and stands out against the background.

Choose an appropriate font: The font you choose should also reflect the tone and mood of your story.

Keep it simple: Don't overcrowd your cover with too many design elements. Instead, focus on one or two key elements that reflect the story.

Create contrast: Use contrast to make your title and image stand out. For example, if you have a light background, use a dark font, and vice versa.

Use negative space: Use negative space to create balance and draw attention to key design elements.

Use symbolism: Consider using symbolism to represent themes or ideas from your story.

Research the market: Look at current trends in the romance book market and try to incorporate them into your design.

Test your cover: Show your cover to a group of people and get feedback on what they like and don't like.

Think about the thumbnail: Keep in mind that your cover will be displayed as a small thumbnail online, so make sure it still looks good at a small size.

Use a professional designer: Consider hiring a professional book cover designer to create your cover.

We give you trusted companies in our 'How To Write a Winning Fiction Book Outline – Romance Workbook'

Avoid stock images: Try to avoid using generic stock images that can be found on many other book covers.

Create a strong focal point: Use a focal point to draw attention to the most important design element on your cover.

Keep it relevant: Make sure your cover reflects the story and characters in your book.

Use typography creatively: Try to use typography in interesting and creative ways to make your cover stand out.

Consider the series: If you're writing a series, make sure your covers have a consistent look and feel.

Don't be afraid to experiment: Don't be afraid to try new things and take risks with your cover design, as long as it still reflects the tone and mood of your story.

There are several common symbols that are often used on romance book covers. Here are a few examples:

Hearts: The heart symbol is a classic representation of love, and it is often used on romance book covers to signal that the book is a love story.

Roses: Roses are a traditional symbol of love and romance, and they are often used on book covers in the romance genre to signify a love story.

Couples: Romance book covers often feature images of couples embracing or holding hands, as a way to convey the central romance in the story.

Kisses: Images of couples kissing are a popular symbol on romance book covers, as they convey the passion and romance of the story.

Beaches: Many romance novels are set in exotic or romantic locations, and book covers may feature images of beaches or other scenic locations to signal this.

Wedding rings: Wedding rings are a symbol of commitment and love, and they are often used on romance book covers to indicate that the story involves marriage or long-term commitment.

Keys: Keys can represent unlocking secrets, passions or even hearts, making it a symbolic gesture to use on romance book covers.

These symbols can help to communicate the theme of the book and appeal to the reader's emotions, which can lead to more interest in the book and potentially increase sales.

30

Editors

There are several types of book editors, each with their own focus and responsibilities. Here are some of the most common types of book editors:

Developmental editor: A developmental editor focuses on the big picture of your book, helping you shape the story, characters, pacing, and overall structure. They may provide feedback on plot, character development, dialogue, and other aspects of your book's content. Developmental editing can cost anywhere from $0.04 to $0.20 per word.

Line editor: A line editor focuses on the language and writing style of your book. They may suggest revisions to improve sentence structure, grammar, syntax, and word choice. Line editing can cost anywhere from $0.03 to $0.10 per word.

Copy editor: A copy editor focuses on correcting errors in grammar, spelling, and punctuation. They may also check for consistency and ensure that your book adheres to a particular style guide. Copy editing can cost anywhere from $0.01 to $0.05 per word.

Proofreader: A proofreader is the final line of defence before your book goes to print. They check for any remaining errors in grammar, spelling, and punctuation that may have been missed during copy editing. Proofreading can cost anywhere from $0.01 to $0.03 per word.

Book coach: A book coach provides guidance and support throughout the writing process. They can help you with everything from developing your book concept to creating a writing schedule and staying motivated. Book coaching can cost anywhere from $100 to $300 per hour.

The benefits of hiring an editor can include improving the quality of your writing, catching errors and inconsistencies, and helping you refine your book's structure and style. A professional editor can also help you ensure that your book is ready for publication and can help you avoid negative reviews or low sales due to poor writing.

While the cost of hiring an editor can vary depending on the level of editing required and the editor's experience, it is generally a worthwhile investment for authors who are serious about their craft and want to create a high-quality book that will stand out in a competitive market.

Not getting your romance novel edited and proofread by a professional can have several consequences, including:

Errors and inconsistencies: Without a professional editor, your novel may contain errors in grammar, spelling, punctuation, and usage. Inconsistencies in the plot or character development can also arise, which can be confusing for readers and undermine the quality of your work.

Poor readability: A romance novel that has not been professionally edited or proofread can be difficult to read. This can lead to a negative reading experience for your audience and may result in bad reviews or lack of interest in your work.

Missed opportunities: A professional editor can help you identify areas where your novel could be improved, whether it's through better pacing, more effective dialogue, or stronger character development. Without an editor, you may miss out on these opportunities to make your work truly shine.

Damage to your reputation: If your novel contains numerous errors or inconsistencies, readers may view you as unprofessional or inexperienced. This can harm your reputation as an author and may make it more difficult for you to sell future books.

In summary, not getting your romance novel edited and proofread by a professional can lead to a number of negative consequences, including errors and inconsistencies, poor readability, missed opportunities for improvement, and damage to your reputation as an author.

Investing in professional editing and proofreading can help ensure that your work is of the highest quality and is well-received by your audience.

We offer a very generous discount in the back of our *'How To Write a Winning Fiction Book Outline – Romance Workbook'* for the editors and proof-reader we use personally in our fiction books.

31

Book Marketing

Here are some free and paid book marketing tips for a romance author:

Free marketing tips:

Social media: Use social media platforms like Twitter, Facebook, and Instagram to connect with your readers and promote your books. Share snippets of your writing, images, and behind-the-scenes glimpses of your writing process.

Here are some specific examples of how you can use social media to promote your romance novel:

Twitter: Share snippets of your writing and quotes from your book on Twitter. Use hashtags relevant to your book and genre, and engage with other authors and readers by responding to their tweets and retweeting their content. For example, you could post a tweet like this: *"I'm so excited to share this excerpt from my new romance novel, XYZ! #romancebooks #amwritingromance #bookexcerpt."*

Facebook: Create a Facebook author page and share behind-the-scenes glimpses of your writing process. This could include photos of your writing space, sneak peeks of upcoming projects, and updates on your writing progress. You can also use Facebook to announce book launches, signings, and other events. For example, you could post a photo of your writing space with a caption like this: *"My writing space is a little messy, but it's where the magic happens! #amwriting #romanceauthor #behindthescenes."*

Instagram: Use Instagram to share visually appealing images that relate to your book and genre. This could include images of book covers, excerpts from your book, or photos that relate to your characters or setting. You can also use Instagram to share short video clips of readings, signings, or other events. For example, you could post an image of your book cover with a caption like this: *"I can't wait for you to fall in love with the characters in my new romance novel, XYZ! #bookstagram #romancereads #bookcoverlove."*

Overall, social media can be a powerful tool for promoting your romance novel. By sharing snippets of your writing, images, and behind-the-scenes glimpses of your writing process, you can connect with readers and build a loyal fan base.

Book bloggers: Reach out to book bloggers and offer them a free copy of your book in exchange for an honest review. Book bloggers often have a dedicated following and can help spread the word about your book.

An example email an author could send to a book blogger:

Subject: Request for Book Review - "Title of Your Book"

Dear [Blogger's Name],

I hope this email finds you well. I recently published a new romance novel, **"Title of Your Book"**, and I came across your blog during my search for reviewers in the genre. I was impressed by your thoughtful reviews and your dedication to promoting new and diverse voices in the book world.

I would be honoured if you would consider reading and reviewing my book. As a thank you for your time and effort, I would be happy to send you a free copy of the book in any format you prefer, whether that's a physical copy, ebook, or audiobook.

"Title of Your Book" is a story about [brief synopsis of the book and what makes it unique]. It has received positive reviews from early readers, and I am confident that it will appeal to your audience of romance readers.

If you are interested in reviewing the book, please let me know and I will be happy to send you a copy. If you have any questions or would like more information, please don't hesitate to reach out.

Thank you for your time and consideration.

Best regards,

[Your Name]

Overall, when reaching out to book bloggers, it's important to be polite, professional, and concise. Offer a free copy of your book, explain what makes it unique, and make it clear that you value their time and expertise.

Goodreads: Set up an author profile on Goodreads and participate in groups and discussions related to your genre. Share your thoughts and connect with other readers and authors.

Email Newsletter: Start an email newsletter and use it to keep your readers updated on new releases, promotions, and upcoming events.

Here's an example of an email promoting a romance novel to your email subscribers:

Subject: New Romance Novel Alert - "Title of Your Book"

Dear [Reader's Name],

I am thrilled to announce the release of my latest romance novel, **"Title of Your Book"**! This book has been a labour of love for me, and I can't wait for you to read it.

"Title of Your Book" is a [brief description of the book and what makes it unique]. I poured my heart and soul into this story, and I am excited to share it with you.

To celebrate the launch of the book, I am offering a special promotion exclusively for my email subscribers. For a limited time, you can purchase the ebook for [discounted price] on all major retailers. I hope this offer encourages you to pick up a copy and experience the love story for yourself.

Additionally, I will be hosting a virtual book launch event on [date and time]. This event will include a live Q&A, readings from the book, and a chance to connect with other romance readers. I would love for you to join me! RSVP [here] to receive the event link.

As always, thank you for your support and enthusiasm for my writing. Your encouragement means the world to me. If you have any questions or feedback, please don't hesitate to reach out.

Warmly,

[Your Name]

Overall, when promoting your romance novel to email subscribers, it's important to make the email personal, engaging, and exciting. Offer a special promotion or event that makes your subscribers feel valued, and highlight what makes your book unique and worth reading. Be sure to include a call-to-action that encourages readers to purchase the book or RSVP to the event.

Book launch event: Organise a book launch event at a local bookstore, library, or community centre. Invite your friends, family, and fans to attend and promote the event on social media.

Here's an example email you could send to a library to ask if you can host a book launch there:

Subject: Request to Host Book Launch at [Library Name]

Dear [Library Contact],

I hope this email finds you well. My name is [Your Name], and I am a local romance author. I recently published my latest book, **"Title of Your Book"**, and I am planning a book launch event in the coming weeks.

I would be honoured if I could host the event at [Library Name]. Your library is a cornerstone of our community, and I believe it would be the perfect venue to celebrate the release of my book.

The event would take place on [date and time]. I would provide copies of the book for sale, and would be happy to sign copies for attendees. I am also planning to give a brief talk about the book and my writing process, and would be happy to answer any questions from the audience.

I understand that your library is likely very busy, but I believe that this event would be a great opportunity to promote reading and local authors. I would be happy to work with you to ensure that the event is well-organised and respectful of library policies.

If you have any questions or concerns, or if you need more information from me, please don't hesitate to reach out. Thank you for your time and consideration, and I hope to hear back from you soon.

Best regards,

[Your Name]

Overall, when reaching out to a library to host a book launch, it's important to be professional, respectful, and persuasive. Explain the details of the event and how it will benefit the library and the community, and be willing to work with the library to ensure a successful event.

Paid marketing tips:

Facebook ads: Use Facebook ads to reach a wider audience and promote your books. You can target specific demographics based on age, gender, location, interests, and more.

Here's an example of a Facebook ad copy for a romance book release:

Headline: Fall in Love with **"Title of Your Book"** - A New Romance Novel.

Body text: Are you looking for a heartwarming and captivating romance story?

Look no further than **"Title of your book"** - the latest novel by bestselling author [your name].

Follow the love story of [main character's name] and [love interest's name] as they navigate their way through [brief description of the plot]. Whether you're a die-hard romance fan or simply looking for a great read, **"Title of Your Book"** is the perfect choice. Order now and fall in love with this irresistible new release!

Call to action: Order now.

Image: A high-quality image of your book cover.

Overall, when writing Facebook ad copy for a romance book release, it's important to highlight what makes your book unique and why it's worth reading.

Use emotive language to create an emotional connection with the reader, and keep the ad copy concise and engaging. Be sure to use a high-quality image of your book cover to grab the reader's attention, and include a clear call-to-action that encourages them to purchase the book.

You can also use Facebook's targeting features to reach a specific demographic of readers who are most likely to be interested in your book.

BookBub: BookBub is a popular book discovery platform that offers paid book promotion services to authors. You can promote your book to a targeted audience of readers who are interested in your genre.

Amazon ads: Use Amazon ads to promote your book on Amazon.com. You can target specific keywords and genres to reach readers who are most likely to be interested in your book.

When targeting keywords on Amazon ads to promote a new romance novel, it's important to choose keywords that are relevant to the book's genre and content. Here are some popular keywords to target:

Romance: This is a broad keyword that can be used to target readers who are searching for romance novels in general.

Romantic suspense: If your book includes elements of suspense or mystery, targeting this keyword can help you reach readers who enjoy this sub-genre.

Historical romance: If your book takes place in a specific historical period, targeting this keyword can help you reach readers who are interested in historical romance novels.

Contemporary romance: If your book takes place in the present day, targeting this keyword can help you reach readers who prefer contemporary romance novels.

New Adult romance: If your book features young adult characters who are transitioning to adulthood, targeting this keyword can help you reach readers who enjoy new adult romance novels.

Small town romance: If your book takes place in a small town setting, targeting this keyword can help you reach readers who enjoy small town romance novels.

Second chance romance: If your book features a couple who reunites after a breakup or period of separation, targeting this keyword can help you reach readers who enjoy second chance romance novels.

Billionaire romance: If your book features a wealthy love interest or explores themes of wealth and privilege, targeting this keyword can help you reach readers who enjoy billionaire romance novels.

Paranormal romance: If your book includes supernatural or paranormal elements, targeting this keyword can help you reach readers who enjoy paranormal romance novels.

LGBTQ+ Romance: If your book features LGBTQ+ characters or explores LGBTQ+ themes, targeting this keyword can help you reach readers who are looking for diverse and inclusive romance novels.

Overall, by targeting relevant and popular keywords on Amazon ads, you can increase the visibility of your romance novel and reach a wider audience of readers who are interested in your book's genre and content.

Book trailers: Create a book trailer and promote it on social media and other platforms. Book trailers can be a great way to build excitement and interest in your book.

Book reviews: Paid book review services can help you get your book reviewed by professional reviewers and literary critics. These reviews can be used on your book cover, promotional materials, and online listings to help attract readers.

Overall, there are many free and paid book marketing strategies that can help you promote your romance novel. By combining a mix of these strategies, you can increase your visibility, build your author brand, and connect with readers who will love your work.

Things to avoid

When marketing your romance novel, there are certain things that you should avoid to ensure that your promotional efforts are effective and well-received. Here are some things to avoid:

Spamming: Avoid spamming readers with frequent or irrelevant promotional content. This can turn readers off and make them less likely to engage with your work.

Overselling: Don't oversell your book or make unrealistic claims about its content or quality. This can lead to disappointment and negative reviews from readers.

Negative reviews: Avoid responding to negative reviews in a defensive or confrontational manner. This can harm your reputation as an author and turn readers away from your work.

Plagiarism: Do not plagiarise or use copyrighted material without permission. This can result in legal action and damage your reputation as an author.

Inappropriate content: Avoid using inappropriate or offensive content in your marketing materials. This can alienate readers and harm your reputation as an author.

Lack of engagement: Do not ignore or neglect your audience. Engage with your readers and respond to their feedback and questions. This can help build a loyal fan base and increase your book's visibility.

Poor quality: Ensure that your marketing materials are of high quality and well-crafted. Poor quality images, videos, or other promotional content can harm your reputation as an author and turn readers away from your work.

32

Romance Writing Glossary

Here's an A-Z romance writing glossary:

A - Alpha Male: A dominant, powerful male character in a romance novel.

B - Beta Hero: A male character who is sensitive, caring, and more in touch with his emotions than an alpha male.

C - Chick Lit: A sub-genre of romance that focuses on young, single women and their relationships.

D - Dark Romance: A sub-genre of romance that explores dark and taboo themes, such as violence, power dynamics, or psychological manipulation.

E - Enemies-to-Lovers: A trope in which the two main characters start out as enemies but eventually fall in love.

F - Friends-to-Lovers: A trope in which the two main characters start out as friends but eventually fall in love.

G - Gothic Romance: A sub-genre of romance that features dark and mysterious settings, supernatural elements and melodramatic plots.

H - Happily Ever After: A romantic ending in which the couple ends up together and in love.

I - Insta-love: A trope in which the two main characters fall in love very quickly, often without much build-up or development.

J - Jealousy: A common theme in romance novels, in which one or both of the main characters experiences jealousy over their love interest.

K - Kiss: A key moment in many romance novels, often signalling the beginning of a romantic relationship between the two main characters.

L - Love Triangle: A trope in which one character must choose between two love interests.

M - Marriage of Convenience: A trope in which the two main characters enter into a marriage for practical reasons, but eventually fall in love.

N - New Adult: A sub-genre of romance that focuses on characters who are in their late teens or early twenties.

O - Opposites Attract: A trope in which the two main characters have very different personalities, backgrounds, or beliefs, but are still drawn to each other.

P - Passion: A key element in many romance novels, representing the intense emotional and physical connection between the two main characters.

Q - Quick Read: A term used to describe short, fast-paced romance novels that can be read quickly.

R - Romantic Comedy: A sub-genre of romance that incorporates humour and light-hearted moments.

S - Slow Burn: A trope in which the romance between the two main characters develops slowly over the course of the novel.

T - Trope: A common theme or plot device used in romance novels, such as enemies-to-lovers, friends-to-lovers, or marriage of convenience.

U - Unrequited Love: A theme in which one character loves the other, but the feelings are not reciprocated.

V - Virgin Heroine: A trope in which the female main character is a virgin, often in contrast to the more experienced male love interest.

W - Wedding: A common ending to many romance novels, often symbolising the ultimate union between the two main characters.

X - X-Rated: A term used to describe romance novels with explicit sexual content.

Y - Yearning: A common theme in many romance novels, in which one or both of the main characters longs for the other.

Z - Zany: A term used to describe quirky or eccentric characters often found in romantic comedies.

Want To Get Your Romance Novel Written?

Consider grabbing our 'How to Write a Winning Fiction Book Outline – Romance Workbook'.

Your all-in-one solution to creating a romance novel from scratch and publishing like a pro!

Want to create an emotional masterpiece that will captivate your readers - without the frustration?

"I just can't seem to get past this part of the story. It's like my brain has hit a wall."

Is this you?

We've been there too, and we've got your back!

Say goodbye to writer's block and hello to a variety of prompts designed for romance writing.

Our done-for-you novel outline templates take you through each scene and chapter, providing a clear path to success.

You'll create plot twists like never before and endings that will leave your readers wanting more.

CONTENTS

Introduction	1
PART 1 - THE GENRE BUNDLE - ROMANCE FICTION	8
• Words Most Frequently Used in Bestselling Book Descriptions	11
• Character Names and Roles	14
• Events	18
• Locations	21
• Titles and Subtitles	24
• Do's and Don't's of the Genre	31
• Romance Tropes and Stereotypes	36
• Power Words	40
• More Plot Twists to add to your Ending	43
• Characters Part 2: Developing them Further	50
• The Final Amazing Novel Summary	62
PART 2 - THE COMPLETE PLAN: YOUR NOVEL OUTLINE	66
• Act 1 - Chapters 1-3	69

Our workbook provides you with a winning step-by-step strategy to keep you on track and maintain consistency in your writing.

CONTENTS

- Act 2 - Chapters 4-6 — 81
- Act 3 - Chapters 7-10 — 94
- Word Count — 108

PART 3 - AFTER YOU HAVE WRITTEN YOUR NOVEL — 111

- Synopsis — 112
- Blurb — 116
- Plotting - Useful Tools to help you Further — 123
- Bestselling Book Covers — 125
- Self-Publishing Vs Traditional Publishing — 130
- Advice from a Bestselling Romance Writer — 133
- Bonuses — 136
- Course Offer — 140
- Contact Us — 148
- Index Cards for Planning — 150

You'll never produce a poor novel - guaranteed!

Grab your copy of **'How to Write a Winning Fiction Book Outline – Romance Workbook' TODAY and be full of confidence!**

You've got readers waiting!

www.ingramcontent.com/pod-product-compliance
Lightning Source LLC
Chambersburg PA
CBHW050251120526
44590CB00016B/2305